1000
AIRLINES
IN COLOUR

1000
AIRLINES
IN COLOUR

GERRY MANNING

Airlife
England

Copyright © 1998 Gerry Manning

First published in the U.K. in 1998
by Airlife Publishing Ltd

British Library Cataloguing-in-Publication Data
A catalogue record for this book
is available from the British Library

ISBN 1 85310 899 5

Typeset by Servis Filmsetting Ltd, Manchester, England
Printed in Singapore by Kyodo Printing Co. (S'pore) Pte Ltd

Airlife Publishing Ltd
101 Longden Road, Shrewsbury, SY3 9EB, England

INTRODUCTION

The aim of this book is to show the range of air transport liveries from both yesterday and today together with the variety of aircraft types that have worn the colours. It is not always a look at the most recent markings and the newest types in service; such a volume would be far too heavy on just a few Boeing/Airbus designs. In order to make it more interesting and varied the aeroplanes illustrated can go back up to thirty years with many of these no longer to be seen in common use, if at all.

Airlines have always changed by merging, by taking on a new identity, or by being taken over by another company, as well as by just going out of business, and many of the airlines in these pages fall into the above categories. What follows is an A to Z of carriers, from small air taxi operators through cargo and charter lines to the large mega airlines flying thousands of people daily across the world. The geographical span is the whole world, and many of the air transport operators pictured are from 'new' countries that have emerged, for instance, from the collapse of the old Soviet empire.

It is a regrettable fact that by the time this book is printed many changes will have taken place in the world of civil aviation. I have tried to have the text as up-to-date as possible as it closes for press.

Gerry Manning
Liverpool

ACKNOWLEDGEMENTS

I am indebted to the four contributors of pictures who filled in the gaps in my own travels from their extensive slide collections. They are, in alphabetical order, Bob O'Brian (R.O'B.), Peter Price (P.E.P.), John Smith (J.D.S.), and Steve Williams (S.G.W). Having known them all for many years it was a delight to dip into their slide collections to pick out what to use. Photographs without a credit are my own. Thanks are also due to Keith Crowden, a font of knowledge on airlines, for some of the textual details, and to Mal Aston for the loan of a word processor to write the captions.

Right: America West Airlines is a Phoenix-based schedule carrier flying mainly around the south-west. In recent times a growing number of aircraft have been painted in special colours (see Special Colour Schemes, p. 141). In the original standard colours is N905AW Boeing 757-2S7 (c/n 23567) at home base, September 1988.

Above: APA International Air Douglas DC-6BF N95BL (c/n 45220) arrives from its Santo Domingo base in the Dominican Republic at Miami, Florida, in June 1988. Although a Dominican airline the fleet at the time consisted of just this one cargo DC-6 leased from Bellomy–Lawson, hence the U.S. registration.

Below: N440AD Convair 440 (c/n 447) of **Airways International Inc.** is about to depart from Fort Lauderdale International, August 1986. This Miami-based company mainly uses small aircraft such as Cessna 400s, the Convair being its largest type.

Above: N428CA CASA 212 Srs.200 (c/n 248) of **American Eagle** taxies to take-off at San Juan in Puerto Rico, November 1992. American Eagle is the name used by a number of different contracted airlines feeding traffic to American Airlines main routes. They all use American Eagle colours and AA flight numbers.

Above: Miami-based **Atlantic Gulf** leased this Allison turboprop-powered Convair CV-580 (converted from a piston CV-340) during 1984. It is seen here in store at Tucson, Arizona, in September 1988. The aircraft is N5822 (c/n 54).

Below: Andes Airlines Douglas DC-8-33AF HC-BEI (c/n 45606) arrives at Miami in October 1981. This cargo operator is based in Guayaquil in Ecuador.

Below: Air Cess is a Sharjah, U.A.E.-based airline with its aircraft registered in Liberia; operations started late in 1995. EL-AKO Antonov AN-24RV (c/n 57310206) shows off the carrier's attractive livery at home base, March 1997.

Above: AeroBrasil Cargo is based at São Paulo. Boeing 707-330C PT-TCM (c/n 19317) is seen here in the cargo area at Miami, April 1994.

Above: This Brazilian built Embraer E110P Bandeirante HK2741 (c/n 110380) is operated by **AIRES** – Aerovias de Integración Regional S.A. – of Bogota, Colombia. Seen arriving at the propliner paradise of Villavicencio, November 1992.

Below: The most stylish of all the great propliners has to be the Lockheed Constellation. Illustrated is HI-548CT, a model L-1049F (c/n 4202) of **Aerochago**, landing at Miami on a flight from home base at Santo Domingo in May 1989. The American F.A.A. has since put a block on a number of countries from flying into the U.S.A. because it claims safety standards are not high enough. Most Dominican cargo operators fell foul of this legislation.

Below: N814AA Dassault Falcon 20CC (c/n 31) of **Active Aero Charter Inc.** sits at home base of Detroit–Willow Run, Michigan, awaiting its next cargo run. Detroit, being the home of the American motor industry, requires a large fleet of cargo aircraft of all sizes to move components around the country to keep production lines running.

Below: Arnarflug, also known as Eagle Air, of Iceland leased this Douglas DC-8-61 N954R (c/n 45908) during 1986. It is seen at Stansted, U.K., before delivery in May of that year.

Above: The Curtiss C-46 is one of the great workhorse props of the world. Found now only in the more remote areas, this example, HK1856 (c/n 369), still carries the name of **Aeronorte** and is seen at Bogota in November 1992. In the late 1980s the airline had been renamed Lineas Aereas Suramericanas. Four years on it still awaits a new company name.

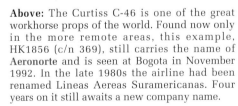

Above: JA8413 Boeing 737-281 (c/n 20507) of **Air Nippon** is seen here on a domestic passenger flight at Fukuoka in May 1992. (*R.O'B.*)

Right: Aero Peru – Empresa de Transport Aereo del Peru – is a passenger operator based in the capital, Lima. Seen arriving at Miami in June 1989 is Douglas DC-8-62 OB-R-1249 (c/n 46132).

Above: ALM Antillean Airlines (Antilliaanse Luchvaart Maatschappij) is based at Curaçao in the Netherlands Antilles. Passenger flights arrive daily in Miami. PJ-SEG McDonnell Douglas MD-82 (c/n 49124) is seen in June 1989 about to depart back home from there.

Below: Lockheed L-1049H Super Constellation HI-542CT (c/n 4825) of **AMSA** (Aerolineas Mundo SA) is seen here at Borinquen, Puerto Rico, November 1992. It is being worked upon to repair the damage caused by being hit by a runaway DC-4. The latter was scrapped.

Above: Venezuelan passenger carrier **Avensa** has a long history, having been founded in 1943. Boeing 737-229 YV-79C (c/n 20908) is photographed at the airline base of Caracas, November 1992.

Above: YV-533C Dornier 228-212 (c/n 8183) of **Aereotuy**, a Venezuelan local operator, is seen at Kavac in November 1992 on a charter to see Angel Falls, the world's highest waterfall.

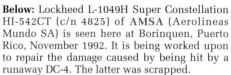

Below: TG-ALA Boeing 727-25C (c/n 19302) of **Aviateca** – Aerolineas de Guatemala – prepares to depart Miami in June 1989 for a flight back to Central America.

Below: Boeing 737 cargo aircraft are not that common. Under charter to **Aviateca – Cargo** is N841LF B737-3S3F (c/n 23811), departing Miami in April 1994. Note the totally different colour scheme to the passenger 727 on the left.

Below: CX-BPL Boeing 707-331C (c/n 19435) of **Aerolineas Uruguayas** lands at Miami, April 1994. The operator of this distinctive colour scheme suspended services at the end of 1994.

Above: On the ramp at Santo Domingo–Las Americas, **Aeromar** Douglas DC-6A HI-592CT (c/n 45110) gets its paintwork touched up; note the masking tape. Photographed in November 1992.

Below: British independent airline **Air UK** operated one of Britain's 'Dakota replacement' designs, the Handley Page HPR7 Herald. G-BEYK, a model 401 (c/n 187), is seen at Liverpool–Speke, April 1983. The only Dakota replacement has proved to be another Dakota.

Above: The Colombian capital of Bogota is the base of Arca – Aerovias Colombianas, a freight operator. Douglas DC-8-53F HK3746X (c/n 45632) lands at Miami, April 1994.

Below: Glinting in the south Florida sun of Miami this **Aero Mexico** Douglas DC-10-30 XA-DUH (c/n 46937) lines up to depart in October 1981.

Above: **Amerijet International** is a Fort Lauderdale, Florida-based freight operator. Seen at Miami in April 1994 is short-bodied Boeing 727-51F N5607 (c/n 18804).

Left: Freight operator **Aeronaves del Peru** Douglas DC-8-55F OB-R-1200 (c/n 45882) seen at Miami, October 1981.

Above: Colombia's main flag carrier is **Avianca**. The airline has been in trouble at various times for the alleged export of drugs hidden in their aircraft. Boeing 707-321C HK-1849 (c/n 18766) is about to depart Miami, October 1981.

Right: Air Jamaica has a very flamboyant colour scheme. N837AB Airbus A310-324 (c/n 674) lands at London–Heathrow, June 1996.

Above: HP-661 Boeing 727-46 (c/n 19280) of **Air Panama** at Miami, October 1981. This Central American operator suspended services in 1990.

Above: Now a rare sight around the world, the Canadair CL44D4s have mostly been withdrawn. October 1981 brought this **AECA** – Aeroservicios Ecuatorianos CA – swing-tail freighter HC-BHS (c/n 14) to Miami.

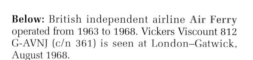

Below: British independent airline **Air Ferry** operated from 1963 to 1968. Vickers Viscount 812 G-AVNJ (c/n 361) is seen at London–Gatwick, August 1968.

Above: Honduran operator **Aero Servicios** – Trans Caribbean Airlines Convair CV-440 HR-ASR (c/n 256) is in store at Kissimmee, Florida, in April 1994 after the airline suspended services in December 1993.

Above: VR-BCX Douglas DC-7C (c/n 45310) of **Arco Bermuda** is seen at Rotterdam in July 1970 loading cargo for Britain during a dock workers strike. The company went out of service in March 1971, and the airframe was broken up at Basle, Switzerland, in 1980.

Below: An international mix. A Czech-built Let 410UVP-E18 (c/n 892313) with a Polish registration, SP-FGK, operated by a Bolivian airline, **AeroSur**. Seen at the airline's home base of Santa Cruz, November 1992.

Below: ALIS – Airline of the Flight Test Formations is a Moscow–Zhukovsky-based carrier supporting the Russian space programme. As this is now only a shadow of its former self the airline can be found earning money on commercial cargo flights. RA76362 Ilyushin IL-76TD (c/n 1033416533) is at Sharjah, U.A.E., March 1997.

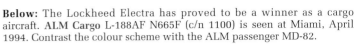

Below: The Lockheed Electra has proved to be a winner as a cargo aircraft. **ALM Cargo** L-188AF N665F (c/n 1100) is seen at Miami, April 1994. Contrast the colour scheme with the ALM passenger MD-82.

Above: **ACES** – Aerolineas Centrales de Colombia – operates both domestic and international services from home base of Medellin. De Havilland (Canada) DHC6 Twin Otter 300 HK2602 (c/n 746) departs from there in November 1992.

Below: **American Airlines** is one of the world's largest carriers for both U.S. internal and international operations. McDonnell Douglas MD-11 N1759 (c/n 48481) arrives at London–Heathrow in October 1993.

Above: **Aeropostal** of Venezuela can lay claim to be the oldest airline in that country, having been founded in 1930. Douglas DC-9-51 YV-22C (c/n 47703) is seen here on the ramp at Caracas in November 1992, the company's home base.

Below: Once a commonplace occurrence at Miami, the propliner is very much in the decline. Local-based cargo carrier **Aerial Transit** Douglas DC-6A N96BL (c/n 43574) arrives in June 1989.

Above: **Alaskan Airlines** is in fact based some way south of that state in Seattle, Washington. McDonnell Douglas MD-83 N932AS (c/n 49233) heads even further south to land at Los Angeles–LAX in September 1988.

Above: N412CA Short SD330-200 (c/n SH3016) of **Allegheny Commuter** on the move at Washington National (D.C.) in May 1989. This airline operated feeder services for U.S. Air using that carrier's flight numbers. Most aircraft have been repainted as U.S. Air Express.

Right: Airpack of Dutch Harbor, Alaska, operated a variety of types from amphibians to four-engine jets. Fairchild F-27F N108AS (c/n 67) is parked at Boeing Field in August 1986.

Above: Air Logistics of Lafayette, Louisiana, is a large user of helicopters dealing with the offshore oil industry. One of the few fixed-wing types operated was this CASA 212-100 N99TF (c/n 89) seen at Boeing Field, Washington, in August 1986.

Below: ATI – Air Transport International – is a freight operator based at Detroit–Willow Run. N8974U Douglas DC-8-62H (c/n 46110) is seen at Opa Locka, Florida, in May 1989. The French flag is visible as the intention was to base the aircraft in Paris.

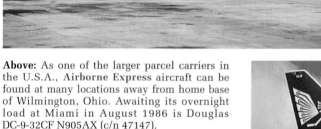

Above: As one of the larger parcel carriers in the U.S.A., Airborne Express aircraft can be found at many locations away from home base of Wilmington, Ohio. Awaiting its overnight load at Miami in August 1986 is Douglas DC-9-32CF N905AX (c/n 47147).

Below: American Trans Air is a major U.S. charter operator with holiday flights to a number of U.K. airfields. N188AT Lockheed L-1011 TriStar 1 (c/n 1078) arrives at Manchester–Ringway in July 1992.

Above: Sri Lanka's flag carrier is AirLanka, based in the capital, Colombo. Lockheed L-1011 TriStar 200 4R-ULM (c/n 1211) arrives at London–Heathrow in September 1993.

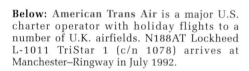

Above: Looking like a fish out of water this Alaskan Coastal Airways Beech C18S N1047B (c/n 7728) sits on the ramp at Renton, Washington, in August 1986. This is not an amphibian and the aircraft will need to be lowered into the water before it can take off again.

Left: Aviation West of Bristol used to fly post and newspapers around the U.K. Britten-Norman BN2A Mk 111 Trislander G-AZLJ (c/n 0319) waits for the night-time departure at Liverpool–Speke in June 1985. The company suspended operations in 1986.

Above: Air Wisconsin Fokker F27 Friendship 500 N504AW (c/n 10677) departs the world's largest airshow at Oshkosh, Wisconsin, in August 1986. The operator now wears the colours of United Express as it feeds customers to that major carrier.

Above: Ameriflight of Burbank, California, has a large fleet of small freight aircraft. N45014 Piper PA31 Navajo (c/n 31-8052171) waits for its next load at Santa Rosa, California, in September 1988.

Below: Air China, based in Beijing, operated this short-body, special performance Boeing 747SP-27 B2454 (c/n 22302) into London–Gatwick in June 1992.

Above: No longer a common sight in the skies of Europe, this **Air Provence** Sud Aviation SE210 Caravelle 12 F-GCVL (c/n 273) arrives at Manchester–Ringway in May 1992.

Above: Associated Air of Paraparaumu, New Zealand, brought one of the two Cessna 402Bs in their fleet to Auckland in May 1986. ZK-DSB (c/n 402B-0585). (*R.O'B.*)

Below: Operating a fleet of propliners the Caracas-based **Aeroejecutivos** has as its largest aircraft this distinctively painted Douglas DC-6A YV-501C (c/n 44645). It is seen at home base in November 1992.

Below: The Central American republic of Costa Rica is home to airline **Aero Costa Rica**. On lease, hence the American registration, is this Boeing 727-225 N354PA (c/n 20624) seen at Miami in November 1992.

Right: AirCal grew quickly in the period following the deregulation of the U.S. airline industry. N464AC Boeing 737-293 (c/n 19309) is seen here at Seattle–Tacoma, Washington, in August 1986. The airline became a prize to be snapped up, and was bought and merged into American Airlines in 1987.

Above: AOM – Air Outre Mer – is a leading French holiday charter airline. F-ODLZ Douglas DC-10-30 (c/n 46869) brings another few hundred to the Greek sunshine as it arrives at Athens in June 1993.

Below: Great colour scheme, pity it didn't last. French charter operator **Aire d'Evasions** had a fleet of just this one Douglas DC-8-73 F-GDRM (c/n 46063), but after only two years suspended operations. The aircraft is seen here about to depart Athens in June 1993.

Above: Seen at Zürich in August 1987 is **Air Holland** Boeing 727-2H3 PH-AHB (c/n 20739). The airline is a major charter carrier.

Above: French airline **Aéromaritime** makes a rare visit to Manchester–Ringway in July 1989. The aeroplane is Boeing 737-33A F-GFUD (c/n 24027).

Below: Bogota-based **Aerotaca** – Aerotaxi Casanare – has a fleet of three de Havilland (Canada) DHC6 Twin Otters. HK2759 (c/n 771) is seen undergoing maintenance at home base in November 1992.

Below: French regional operator **Air Littoral** has an international service to Manchester–Ringway. F-GHIB Embraer E120RT Brasilia (c/n 120162) arrives in July 1993.

Above: Based at Faro in the Algarve region of Portugal, **Air Atlantis** flies holiday charters to the U.K. CS-TCH Boeing 727-232 (c/n 20866) is seen at London–Gatwick in July 1987.

Below: Funchal in Madeira, is a Portuguese possession off the coast of Africa. **Air Columbus**, based here until its suspension of operations in December 1994, flew holidaymakers to various European destinations. CS-TKB Boeing 727-2J4 (c/n 20764) shows off its most attractive colour scheme as it arrives at Manchester–Ringway in April 1991.

Below: Based in Ekaterinburg, Russia, **Aviacon Zitotrans** flies both passenger and cargo services. Operating the former is Tupolev TU-154M RA85671 (c/n 829) seen on a service to Sharjah, U.A.E., in March 1997.

Above: The violent break-up of the old state of Yugoslavia has produced a number of new operators and registration letters. Operating through all the mayhem from its base in the federal capital of Belgrade is **Aviogenex**, who in happier times flew tourists to what is still a beautiful country. YU-AJA Tupolev TU-134A (c/n 1206) is seen about to depart Zürich in August 1987. As with so many operators in eastern Europe, Russian-built equipment has been replaced with western aircraft for economic reasons.

Below: The break-up of the U.S.S.R. has given the airline enthusiast more new airlines and countries than he could have dreamed about. After Russia, the largest operating 'new' country is the Ukraine. It was possible to see on the same day at the same airport two different types of aircraft from two different operators. UR-42544 Yakovlev YAK-42 (c/n 11151004) of **Air Ukraine** is at Manchester–Ringway in July 1993.

Above: ATI – Aero Transporti Italiani – is a subsidiary of Alitalia flying charters. I-ATIQ Douglas DC-9-32 (c/n 47591) is at London–Gatwick in July 1987.

Above: Based in Trieste, **Aligiulia** operated scheduled services from there until flights were suspended in 1986. Seen in store at East Midlands–Castle Donington in June 1986 is the last production Handley Page HPR7 Herald 209 I-ZERD (c/n 197), still in the markings from its lease to the company.

Below: Air Ukraine International was no doubt often confused with Air Ukraine. Perhaps this has led it changing its name to Ukraine International Airlines. From the beginning it has operated western equipment. UR-GAA (note different registration configuration) Boeing 737-4Y0 (c/n 26069) lands at Manchester–Ringway in July 1993.

Below: Aerolineas Argentinas Boeing 747-287B LV-OEP (c/n 22297) lands at London–Heathrow in July 1995 at the end of the long flight from Buenos Aires.

Above: A large aeroplane for a small place, the main resource of the Seychelles being tourism. F-BVGM Airbus A300B4-203 (c/n 078) of **Air Seychelles** is pushed back at London–Gatwick with a load of holidaymakers bound for Mahe, July 1987.

Above: Air Cargo of Liberia Ltd had this Antonov AN32 CCCP-48109 on lease. It is seen at Moscow–Myachikovo in August 1991.

Above: Mexican airline **Aerotur** placed this Convair CV-340 XA-LOU (c/n 120) in store at Opa Locka, Florida. Photographed in August 1986.

Above: Running a regular service between Malta and London–Heathrow, **Air Malta** operates Airbus A320-211 9H-ABP (c/n 112) as part of its fleet. Photographed September 1993.

Below: Out on the edge of the Colombian jungle, Villavicencio is the last outpost of civilisation in the area. It is also a propliner haven. **Aerosol** Curtiss C-46F Commando HK400 (c/n 22468) taxies past the café window in November 1992.

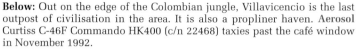

Above: Air Toulouse is one of the last European operators of the Sud Aviation SE210 Caravelle. F-GDJU, a model 10B3 (c/n 183), heads out of London–Gatwick in May 1991. (*J.D.S.*)

Left: Bulgarian carrier **Air Zory** is based in the capital, Sofia. It was founded in 1993 by former Balkan pilot Angel Karamihov who took the airline's title from his daughter's name, Zorinza. LZ-AZC Ilyushin IL-18V (c/n 184006903) is on the ramp at Sharjah, U.A.E., in March 1997.

Above: German airline **Aero Lloyd** is based at Frankfurt. This McDonnell Douglas MD-83 D-ALLF (c/n 49602) is seen at Düsseldorf in July 1996. (*J.D.S.*)

Above: **Avior Airlines** Piper PA31 Navajo VH-RTN (c/n 31-13) is at Melbourne–Essendon, April 1982. The carrier was based at Perth in Western Australia and suspended operations in 1987. (*R.O'B.*)

Below: **Air Pacific** was a commuter operator in California. In early 1980 it merged with Gem State Airlines. Prior to that de Havilland (Canada) DHC7 Dash 7-102 N9058P (c/n 5) waits for passengers at Bakersfield, California, in October 1979.

Above: **Airlift** was one of the great names in American cargo operators, founded in 1945. N108RD Douglas DC-8-54F (c/n 45663) is seen at Miami in October 1981. In 1992 the airline suspended operations.

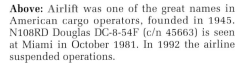

Above: The Martin 404 is no longer in passenger service. **Air Florida Commuter** N259S (c/n 14233) is on the ramp at Miami, October 1981.

Below: **Air Florida** Douglas DC-10-30 N1035F (c/n 46992) lands at its home base of Miami in October 1981. The airline merged with Midway and this aeroplane went to Fed-Ex.

Below: This Curtiss C-46D Commando HI-602CA (c/n 33379) was the total fleet of **Antillas Air Cargo**, seen at the home base of Santo Domingo, Dominican Republic, November 1992. The following year the company ceased flying.

Right: Once a mixed passenger and cargo airline, **Arrow Air** of Miami now just flies freight. N8968U Douglas DC-8-62F (c/n 46069) heads for the cargo sheds at base in April 1994.

Above: The name 'Air Atlantic' crops up a number of times with totally different operators in different countries. This one is **Air Atlantic Cargo**, a Nigerian company. Boeing 707-369C 5N-TNO (c/n 20085) is seen at Ostend, Belgium, in July 1996. (*P.E.P.*)

Below: American International Airways Douglas DC-8-61F N812CK (c/n 45890) departs Miami in April 1994. Based at Detroit–Willow Run, it is owned and managed by former drag racing star Connie Kalitta. The company is now one of the fastest-growing cargo airlines in America.

Above: Argosy Airlines Douglas DC-3 Dakota N14931 (c/n 2118), seen at Opa Locka, Florida, in October 1981. The operator, based at Fort Lauderdale, used a fleet of four Dakotas in the mid-1970s. Routes flown included a regular service to the Bahamas.

Above: N471GB Boeing 737-159 (c/n 19680) of **Air California** is at San Francisco–S.F.O. in October 1979. The name was later changed to Air Cal.

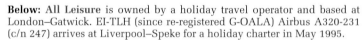

Below: Aliansa of Villavicencio in Colombia operates a fleet of three cargo Dakotas. Seen at base in November 1992 is Douglas DC-3 HK140 (c/n 6344).

Below: All Leisure is owned by a holiday travel operator and based at London–Gatwick. EI-TLH (since re-registered G-OALA) Airbus A320-231 (c/n 247) arrives at Liverpool–Speke for a holiday charter in May 1995.

Above: Aerobol – Aerovias Bolivar – flies a variety of small types from Ciudad Bolivar in central Venezuela. YV-270C Britten–Norman BN2A Islander (c/n 573) waits at base for its next load in November 1992.

Left: Based in Savannah, Georgia, **Av Atlantic** runs a fleet of seven Boeings. N203AV 727-259 (c/n 22474) moves out of Miami in April 1994.

Below: The NAMC YS-11A-213 is a Japanese-built airliner powered by a pair of Rolls-Royce Dart turboprops. **All Nippon Airways** operated JA9734 (c/n 2103), seen here at Tokyo–Haneda in May 1977. (*R.O'B.*)

Below: Besides a fleet of five Dakotas, **Atorie Air** of El Paso, Texas, operated this attractively painted Curtiss C-46F Commando N800FA (c/n 22595) named *Condor*. It is seen at Tucson, Arizona, in October 1984.

Above: Air Colombia works with the oil industry in that country. Douglas DC-3 Dakota HK3292 (c/n 19661) departs Bogota in November 1992 with a consignment of pipes for drilling.

Below: ASA – Atlantic Southeast Airlines – now mostly wears the colours of Delta Connection and feeds that carrier's hubs. Seen in its own colours Embraer E120ER Brasilia N265AS (c/n 120170) is at Macon, Georgia, in April 1994.

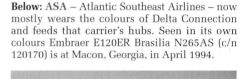

Below: The Aviation Traders ATL98 Carvair is basically a Douglas DC-4 with a whole new large nose and a front opening cargo door. They first operated in the early 1960s and were used for the carriage of cars across the English Channel. Twenty-one airframes were converted and only a handful are still to be found active. **Academy Airlines** of Griffin, Georgia, operated two. N83FA (c/n 10365/5) is seen undergoing maintenance at base in April 1994. As with many cargo aircraft the colour scheme is of low importance.

Below: I-GISI Sud Aviation SE210 Caravelle 10B-3 (c/n 188) of the Italian charter operator **Altair** is at Luton, U.K., September 1984. (*J.D.S.*)

Right: Mexican freight operator **Aero Pacifico**, based at La Paz, had XA-PII Boeing C97G (c/n 17149) painted and prepared for them at Tucson in October 1992. They suspended operations the same year. (*J.D.S.*)

Above: **Arkia** – Israel Inland Airways – operated this Vickers Viscount 831 4X-AVG (c/n 419) from 1974 to 1982 when it was sold in the U.S.A. Seen here at Tucson, Arizona, in store, still in livery, in October 1984.

Below: **Air India** operates that country's services to the U.K. VT-ESN Boeing 747-437 (c/n 27164) lands at London–Heathrow in July 1995.

Above: New Zealand's flag carrier is **Air New Zealand**. Boeing 737-2Y5 ZK-NAF (c/n 23038) is seen at Melbourne–Tullimarine in Australia in October 1996. (*R.O'B.*)

Above: **Air Hong Kong** operates a regular cargo service between Hong Kong and Manchester–Ringway. VR-HME Boeing 747-265B (c/n 22106) lands at Manchester, June 1996.

Below: Douglas DC-9-31 P4-MDD (c/n 47271) of **Air Aruba** lifts off from Miami, April 1994.

Below: Perth-based **Air W.A.** (Western Australia) have since merged into Ansett, Australia's largest internal airline. BAe 146-200 G-WAUS (c/n E2008) is seen in the company colours at the Farnborough Air Show, September 1984.

Below: Antilles Air Boats of St Croix in the Virgin Islands must have been the last operator, flying passengers, of four-engine flying boats in the world. Short S25 Sandringham VP-LVE (c/n SB2018) is seen here on Lough Derg, Killaloe, in Ireland, August 1977. It was in the country to operate pleasure flights to the Arran Islands. This magnificent aircraft is now preserved in a museum in the U.K.

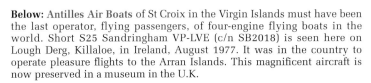

Above: The political changes following the civil war in the Yemen meant that two different airline liveries operated into the U.K. Leased Airbus A310-304 F-ODSV (c/n 473) in the colours of **Alyemen**, the airline for South Yemen, arrives at London–Heathrow in July 1995. The airline was merged into Yemenia in May 1996.

Below: Air Liberté Douglas DC-10-30 F-GPVE (c/n 46981) is normally seen operating far-flung holiday charters from France. The French football team playing in Manchester brought it to the U.K. in June 1996 with supporters. The airline went into receivership in September 1996. It was still operating most flights and looking for a buyer.

Above: French scheduled operator **Air Inter** brings Airbus A330-301 F-GMDB (c/n 037) into Manchester–Ringway on a charter in June 1996 with a full load of football fans for the Euro '96 competition. The company have been taken over by Air France and the name changed to Air Inter Europe.

Below: Ariana Afghan Airlines has operated this short-body Boeing 727-113C YA-FAU (c/n 20343) since new in January 1970. It is operated in a combi, i.e. both passenger and freight role. It is seen here at Sharjah, U.A.E., in March 1997 being loaded with thousands of cassette recorders.

Above: Air 2000 is a well respected holiday charter operator in the U.K. Boeing 757-225 G-OOOW (c/n 22611) lands at Manchester–Ringway in March 1997 in the new livery introduced late the previous year.

Above: Lisbon-based **Air Sul** Boeing 737-2K5 CS-TMD (c/n 22599) is at Manchester–Ringway in June 1991. Operations were suspended in January the following year. (*J.D.S.*)

Right: Following the take-over of Air Inter by Air France the fleet is being repainted in the new name of **Air Inter Europe**. Airbus A320-111 F-GGEB (c/n 12) arrives at London–Heathrow in June 1996 in the new livery.

Above: **Aer Lingus**, the Irish flag carrier, has replaced its 747s with Airbus A330-301s for the long-haul transatlantic routes. EI-DUB (c/n 55) departs the company base, Dublin, in June 1994.

Left: The national airline of Italy is **Alitalia**. It flies scheduled services worldwide. Airbus A300B4-203 I-BUSF (c/n 123) taxies into a gate at Rome–Fiumicino, June 1988.

Above: In recent years Swedish operator **Air Ops** has specialised in leasing back-up aircraft to charter carriers. Lockheed L-1011 TriStar 100 SE-DSD (c/n 1215) is on tow at Manchester–Ringway in May 1996.

Below: For most of the 1960s **Austrian Airlines**, the national flag carrier, operated this Vickers Viscount 837 OE-IAM (c/n 442) on passenger services around Europe. Seen here at London–Gatwick, August 1968.

Below: The break-up of Yugoslavia has produced the new country of Slovenia. Existing Inex Adria Airlines had a name change, a colour scheme change and a registration letter change. S5-AAB Airbus A320-231 (c/n 113) of **Adria** lands at London–Heathrow in July 1995.

Above: This **Air Atlanta** has no connections with the American city; it is an Icelandic passenger charter airline. Lockheed L-1011 TriStar 1 TF-ABH (c/n 1054) lands at Manchester–Ringway in June 1996.

Below: **AMAZ** (Agence et Messageries Aérienne du Zaïre), based in Kinshasa, bought this ex-Royal Air Force Bristol 175 Britannia 253 9Q-CAJ (c/n 13511) in November 1975. Due to financial problems the sale fell through. It is seen at Luton, U.K., September 1976. (*J.D.S.*)

Below: With a very distinctive colour scheme **Air Spain** Douglas DC-8-21 EC-CDA (c/n 45429) climbs out of Palma, Majorca, in November 1973. The airline flew holiday charters.

Left: I-TRAM Britten-Norman BN2 Islander (c/n 8) of Pisa-based **Aertirrena** is seen at Ford, U.K., August 1970.

Below: Spanish charter operator **Aviaco** has been flying holidaymakers to and from Spain for many years. Sud Aviation SE210 Caravelle VI.R EC-ARI (c/n 107) lands at Palma, Majorca, November 1973.

Below: Landing at Manchester–Ringway in March 1994 is EC-FJR Boeing 737-3Y0 (c/n 24462) of the Spanish holiday charter operator **Air Europa**.

Left: At one time any civil aircraft in the U.S.S.R. was listed as belonging to **Aeroflot**. The break-up of that nation has produced a growth of airlines of all types. This picture is from the days of the U.S.S.R. SSSR (CCCP in Cyrillic script) 42397 Tupolev TU-104A is seen at Schiphol, Amsterdam, July 1970.

Above: **AJT Air International** (Asian Joint Transport) is yet another of Russia's new operators. Ilyushin IL-86 RA86115 (c/n 5148320983) departs Sharjah on a flight back home to Moscow, March 1997. It is operating the flight on behalf of Aeroflot; note its titles on the nose.

Below: Just to show not all things changed with the U.S.S.R. break-up, this Antonov AN-22 RA09328 is marked as **Aeroflot** but operated by the Ministry of Defence. (Note the fresh paint where the CCCP registration has been replaced with the new Russian republic letters of RA) It is seen at Moscow–Domodedovo, August 1995.

Below: **Aviaenergo** is one of the new names to be seen on the ramps of Russian airports. It operates a mixed fleet of passenger and cargo aircraft. It includes a single example of an Antonov AN-74 RA74040 (c/n 36547097930) at Moscow–Domodedovo in August 1995.

Right: This Antonov AN-12 CCCP 11118 (c/n 1348002) carries the name of **Aerocomplex**, a Dubai-based cargo airline associated with Aeroflot. The latter supplied all the aircraft with only the name changed. It is seen in August 1991 at Leningrad–Pulkovo.

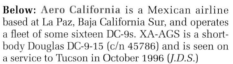

Above: Georgia is another ex-U.S.S.R. new country with new registration letters. 4L-65061 Tupolev TU-134A-3 (c/n 49874) of **Adjal Avia** is seen arriving at Moscow–Vnukovo in August 1995.

Below: Aero California is a Mexican airline based at La Paz, Baja California Sur, and operates a fleet of some sixteen DC-9s. XA-AGS is a short-body Douglas DC-9-15 (c/n 45786) and is seen on a service to Tucson in October 1996 (*J.D.S.*)

Above: Being brought into service by Hamilton Aviation at Tucson in October 1996 was this Lockheed L-1011 TriStar 100 SE-DPR (c/n 1231) for **Time Air Sweden**. (*J.D.S.*)

Above: AirWorld are owned by a holiday travel company and operate seasonally. G-BVZU Airbus A320-231 (c/n 280) arrives at Manchester–Ringway in August 1995.

Below: Air Club is a Canadian airline flying charters to the U.K. as well as other countries. C-GCIV Airbus A310-324 (c/n 451) approaches to land at Manchester–Ringway, September 1996.

Below: Based in French-speaking Montreal **Air Transat** flies charters to various European destinations. Lockheed L-1011 TriStar 1 C-GTSZ (c/n 1103) arrives at Athens in June 1993.

Below: **Air BC** operates commuter flights around the province of British Columbia. Seen receiving attention at its Vancouver base is C-FPAE de Havilland (Canada) DHC6 Twin Otter 200 (c/n 228) in September 1984.

Above: This Consolidated PBY-5A Canso C-FJCV (c/n CV357) was the sole aircraft in the fleet of **Air Caledonia**, based at Vancouver, British Columbia. It was later sold to Africa where it operated air cruises, and since then it has moved on to New Zealand. Photo Vancouver, September 1984.

Below: **Angola Airlines** (Linhas Aereas de Angola) Lockheed L-1011 TriStar 500 CS-TEC (c/n 1241) arrives at Moscow–Sheremetyevo 2 after a flight from Luanda in September 1995. The aircraft is on lease from TAP – Air Portugal, hence the registration.

Above: One of the two major international scheduled airlines in its home land, **Air Canada** Boeing 747-133 C-FTOC (c/n 20015) lands at London–Heathrow in July 1995. This is the current livery; contrast this with the older colours of the Air Canada Cargo Express DC-8.

Below: Operating a cargo service from the Zimbabwe capital of Harare to London–Gatwick comes this Douglas DC-8F-55 Z-WMJ (c/n 45821) of **Affretair** in June 1995. It is interesting to note that the Zimbabwe registration consists of just four alphabetical characters; all other countries using just the alphabet have at least five characters.

Above: Mali is one of those forgotten countries in north central Africa. **Air Mali**, the national airline, is based at Bamako. Ilyushin IL-18B TZ-ABE (c/n 3304) is seen at Paris–Le Bourget in May 1971.

Above: Russian cargo airline **Aviatrans** is yet another new carrier. RA11901 Antonov AN-12 (c/n 1340103) sits at its base of Moscow–Myachikovo in August 1995.

Right: Paris-based carrier **Air Jet** operates a fleet of three 146s in both passenger and cargo roles. Seen flying people into Liverpool–Speke in June 1996 for a football game is F-GOMA BAe 146-200 (c/n E2211).

Above: Algeria's only airline is **Air Algérie**. Boeing 727-2D6 7T-VEW (c/n 22375) operates passenger services. It is seen landing at London–Heathrow in July 1995.

Below: About to depart from Moscow–Vnukovo airport in August 1995 is this **Adjarian Airlines** Tupolev TU-134A-3 UR65877 (c/n 31250). This is a co-operation between former U.S.S.R. republics as the registration and flag are Ukrainian but the airline is Georgian.

Above: Air Botswana Cargo operated this Lockheed L-100-30 Hercules A2-ACA (c/n 35C-4701). It is to be found here a long way from home on a sub-lease at Liverpool–Speke in May 1984.

Below: ATO – Air Transport Office – of Kinshasa, Zaire (now known as the Democratic Republic of Congo), leased this Ilyushin IL-18D RA75466 (c/n 187010403) from Gosnii, Georgia. As can be seen not a vast amount of money went into the repaint for the lease. Photo at Moscow–Sheremetyevo 1, September 1995.

Above: 'UN' is the registration letter for the republic of Kazakhstan, an ex-U.S.S.R. country. This example is UN86130, an Ilyushin IL-62M (c/n 3255333) of **Aral Air**; it is on the ramp at Moscow–Zhukovsky in August 1995.

Above: Aero Lik is based at Moscow–Bykovo and operates three Yakovlev YAK-40s together with a single IL-18. This YAK-40 RA87814 (c/n 9230524) is seen at home base waiting the next load of passengers.

Left: The Boeing 747 freighter has a nose door that hinges upwards; the other major point of reference is the complete lack of cabin windows. **Air France Cargo** Boeing 747-228F F-GCBK (c/n 24158) is seen at London–Heathrow in June 1992.

Above: **Aer Arran**, based at Connemara in Ireland, has operated this Britten-Norman BN2A-8 Islander EI-AYN (c/n 704) for many years. It is seen here at Liverpool–Speke in April 1986 on a charter flight with horse racing fans for the Grand National.

Below: Seen landing at Athens in June 1993 with a full load of British holidaymakers is Boeing 757-236 G-BUDX (c/n 25592) of **Ambassador Airways**. This British charter company suspended services in November the following year.

Above: In a colour scheme very similar to Dan Air, who supplied the aeroplane, this **Aberdeen Airways** Avro (HS) 748-245 Srs2 G-BFLL (c/n 1658) is parked at East Midlands–Castle Donington in July 1991. The airline suspended operations in November 1992.

Above: **Aer Lingus Commuter** is a division of Aer Lingus. During the period 1984 to 1992 they operated this Short SD360 EI-BEK (c/n SH3635). It is seen here on a regular scheduled passenger service to Liverpool–Speke in April 1986.

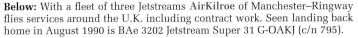

Below: **Air Namibia** of south-west Africa operates this Beech 1900C V5-LTB (c/n UB-29) on services from the capital Windhoek to Durban in South Africa. It is seen at the latter in April 1993. (*R.O'B.*)

Below: With a fleet of three Jetstreams **AirKilroe** of Manchester–Ringway flies services around the U.K. including contract work. Seen landing back home in August 1990 is BAe 3202 Jetstream Super 31 G-OAKJ (c/n 795).

Right: Air Europe grew to be a very large player in the U.K. holiday charter market. It ceased to trade in March 1991. (Compare the colours to that of Air Europa of Spain, who continue to fly.) G-BLVH Boeing 757-236 (c/n 23227) is seen at Manchester–Ringway in April 1987.

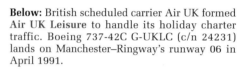

Above: In July 1980 this most attractively painted Boeing 707-331 N762TW (c/n 17674) could be found operating **Air Tanzania's** service from Dar-es-Salaam to London–Gatwick. It is photographed at the latter. (*J.D.S.*)

Below: British scheduled carrier Air UK formed **Air UK Leisure** to handle its holiday charter traffic. Boeing 737-42C G-UKLC (c/n 24231) lands on Manchester–Ringway's runway 06 in April 1991.

Above: Air Europe Express operated scheduled commuter services within the U.K. When the parent company folded, so did the airline. Short SD360 G-BLRT (c/n SH3661) lands at Manchester–Ringway in 1990.

Above: During the mid-1980s Wales could claim to have its own airline, **Airways International Cymru** (Cymru is Wales in the Welsh language); however it ceased trading in January 1988. Seen at London–Gatwick in July 1987 is Boeing 737-204 G-BAZI (c/n 20808).

Below: ABC – Air Bridge Carriers Ltd – was one of the few civil operators of the Armstrong Whitworth Argosy. This versatile freight design, with both a nose and tail door, is seen waiting for an overnight newspaper run at Liverpool–Speke in April 1982. G-APRL Model 101 (c/n 6652) ended its days preserved in a museum at Coventry in the U.K.

Below: In the mid-1980s ABC introduced a much smarter colour scheme and shortened the company name to **Air Bridge**. Seen here in July 1991 at home base of East Midlands–Castle Donington is Vickers Merchantman 953C G-APEP (c/n 719). The Merchantman was a cargo conversion of the Vanguard airliner. The last Merchantman was in service until the end of 1996 when it was retired to a museum at its birthplace of Wisley.

Below: When the tall-tailed Super Dakota was introduced to the world's airlines the total sale was just three! The reason was not the product, but that too many ordinary Dakotas were available far cheaper from surplus war stocks. The saving grace for the type was the U.S. Navy who bought 100 R4D-8s (later C-117s). When they were phased out of service in the mid-1970s after storage they became an attractive proposition with their low hours and excellent maintenance records. **Air 500** of Toronto operated this Douglas C-117D C-FALL (c/n 43385) for four years from 1988. It is seen at base in June 1990.

Below: Before they became an Air Canada Connector and took that company's colours, **Air Ontario** flew the Convair CV-580 on services around Canada. C-GGWI (c/n 169) arrives at Toronto in July 1986.

Below: Air Manitoba will fly anything around the province that will fit into their aircraft. Until recently they operated a number of very smart Douglas DC-3 Dakotas from their base at Winnipeg. C-GSCC (c/n 33352) awaits a passenger load at base in June 1990.

Above: Ontario-based **Air Creebec** fly both passengers and freight around the northern parts of Canada's richest province. Avro (HS) 748-214 Srs2A C-GMAA (c/n 1576) is photographed at Pickle Lake in June 1990. It should be noted that the pressurisation system in this freight aircraft has been deactivated to increase airframe life.

Above: This **Air Canada Cargo Express** Douglas DC-8-63AF C-FTIU (c/n 46113) arrives at Zürich in August 1987. It carries the colour scheme that has now been supplanted.

Above: Before the current policy of just operating commuter-size aircraft, and a name change to Equator Airlines, **African Express Airways** of Nairobi, Kenya, flew large jets. Boeing 707-351C 5Y-AXC (c/n 18746) is seen undergoing maintenance at Stansted, U.K., in May 1987.

Below: A number of major European airlines have started an 'Asia' subsidiary so that they can operate to both China and Taiwan without upsetting the former. Seen landing at Dubai, U.A.E., in March 1997 is **Air France Cargo Asie** Boeing 747-228C F-GCBH (c/n 23611). Note that the tail marks are all in one colour and do not have the red of the parent company.

Above: Seen on the ramp at Cairo in June 1988 is Boeing 737-266 SU-AYO (c/n 21227) of Egyptian domestic operator **Air Sinai**.

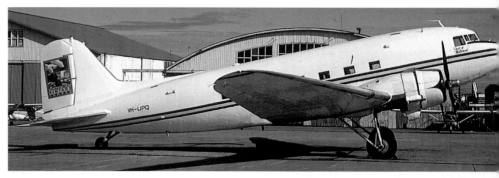

Right: The rudder markings on this Douglas DC-3 Dakota reveal it belongs to **Australian Vintage Travel**. VH-UPQ (c/n 33300) is seen at Melbourne–Essendon in July 1987. Regrettably the vintage travel did not succeed and the aeroplane moved to fly freight for Rebel Air at Sydney. (*R.O'B.*)

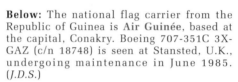

Above: **Air Caledonie International** is based at Noumea, New Caledonia, a French possession in the south Pacific. F-GEPC Sud Aviation SE210 10B-3 (c/n 184) is seen on a visit to Sydney–Mascot, Australia, in April 1988. (*R.O'B.*)

Below: The national flag carrier from the Republic of Guinea is **Air Guinée**, based at the capital, Conakry. Boeing 707-351C 3X-GAZ (c/n 18748) is seen at Stansted, U.K., undergoing maintenance in June 1985. (*J.D.S.*)

Above: Australian freight carrier **Air Express** operated three aircraft when it suspended services in 1979. Two were DC-4s, the other was this Bristol B170 Freighter Mk31M VH-ADL (c/n 13193). It is seen in store at Melbourne–Essendon in June 1983. (*R.O'B.*)

Above: Seen in store at Marana, Arizona, during October 1976 is this **Air South** Fairchild F-27J N2705J (c/n 116). The airline was taken over by Air Florida. (*S.G.W.*)

Below: British charter operator **Air Bristol** has a fleet of three BAC 111s. Seen in May 1995 at Stansted is BAC 111-510ED G-AVMW (c/n 150). (*S.G.W.*)

Below: **Austral** is an Argentinian scheduled passenger airline based at Buenos Aires Aeroparque. Douglas DC-9-32 LV-WIS (c/n 47312) is seen departing base, November 1995. (*R.O'B.*)

Below: **Air Mauritius** is the flag carrier for that country. 3B-NAL Boeing 767-23B (c/n 23974) is seen in November 1993 at Harare, Zimbabwe. (*R.O'B.*)

Above: Scottish airline **Air Ecosse** operated an aircraft share deal with Fairflight. Short SD330-200 G-BKSV (c/n SH3096) is seen about to depart Liverpool–Speke in April 1984.

Below: What was formally Air Rhodesia was renamed **Air Zimbabwe** after independence. Vickers Viscount 748D Z-YNB (c/n 99) is seen at the nation's capital, Harare, in April 1993. (*R.O'B.*)

Below: Air Tran is an Orlando, Florida-based passenger operator. N461AT Boeing 737-2E1 (c/n 20976) is seen at base in October 1995. (*J.D.S.*)

Right: Israeli local operators are not usually to be found as far away as Moscow–Sheremetyevo 1. Yet August 1995 saw the arrival of **Aeroel Airways** Grumman G159 Gulfstream 1 4X-ARV (c/n 101). The airline is owned by the French carrier Air Provence International. (*J.D.S.*)

Below: Short-lived holiday charter company **Air Manchester** began operations in May 1982 with this BAC 111-416 G-SURE (c/n 129). It is seen departing home base of Manchester–Ringway in September 1982. The carrier was a division of Manchester-based Sureway Travel; services were suspended in 1983. (*J.D.S.*)

Above: Air Afrique is one of only a few multinational state airlines. It covers eleven countries of sub-Saharan Africa; all are ex-French colonies. The H.Q. is Abidjan in the Ivory Coast. TU-TAE Airbus A310-308 (c/n 652) is seen at London–Gatwick, September 1994. (*J.D.S.*)

Right: The last design from the old historic French aircraft manufacturer Potez, before the factory was taken over by Sud Aviation, was the Potez 840, a sixteen to twenty-four seat feedliner. It failed to sell and only eight airframes including prototypes and static tests were built. Seen in a hangar at Munich–Reim in July 1968 is the first production Potez 841 D-CAER (c/n 1) in the colours of **Aero Dienst**. This company still trades today as an executive charter operator based at Nuremburg. (*S.G.W.*)

Above: **Air Anglia** was formed in 1970 by the merger of three eastern English companies. They flew both charter and scheduled services. Douglas DC-3 Dakota G-AOBN (c/n 11711) is at Liverpool–Speke in March 1973 for a charter flight.

Below: The airline of the U.K. colony of the British Virgin Islands, until its suspension in June 1991, was **Air BVI** Douglas DC-3 Dakota VP-LVJ (c/n 9795) is seen at Antigua in June 1983. (*R.O'B.*)

Above: **Airtours** is one of the U.K.'s largest holiday charter airlines. Seen on tow at Manchester–Ringway in June 1996 is Boeing 767-31K G-SJMC (c/n 27205).

Above: Seen at Luton, U.K., in May 1979 at the end of its life following four years with Dubai-based **Air Faisal**, a cargo airline, is G-BDLZ Bristol 175 Britannia 253 (c/n 13435). The colour scheme is basic Royal Air Force, its previous owner. The carrier flew services from its base to Bombay as well as other Indian cities until it closed down in 1979.

Below: Based at the capital city of Brussels is **Air Belgium**, a small passenger airline. OO-ABB Boeing 737-2P6 (c/n 21359) is visiting Manchester–Ringway in April 1980. (*J.D.S.*)

Below: Turkish operator **Air Alfa** flies five Airbus aircraft. TC-ALS A300B4K-103 (c/n 066) arrives at Düsseldorf in July 1996. (*P.E.P.*)

Below: AVI – Aero Virgin Islands – is based on the U.S. Virgin Island of St Thomas. Seen at base is this Douglas DC-3 Dakota N5117X (c/n 6054) in April 1989. (*S.G.W.*)

Above: **Air Ceylon** used to be the flag carrier for the island of Ceylon off the southern coast of India. After independence from the U.K. the country was renamed Sri Lanka. Air Ceylon suspended operations at the end of the 1970s. De Havilland DH121 Trident 1E-140 4R-ACN (c/n 2135) is seen prior to delivery at the Paris air show, Le Bourget, June 1969. (*S.G.W.*)

Below: Airlines are not seen at airshows very often. Seen at the International Air Tattoo at Fairford, U.K., in July 1991 is **Anglo Cargo** Boeing 707-338C G-BDEA (c/n 19296). It was at the show in recognition of the work the company had performed in hauling cargo during the Gulf War earlier that year. Sad to report the company suspended operations in January the following year. (*S.G.W.*)

Above: The former French African colony of Gabon, now the Gabonese Republic, has **Air Gabon** as the national flag carrier. Boeing 747-2Q2B F-ODJG (c/n 21468) is seen on approach to London–Gatwick in September 1996. The aircraft was bought new but has always had a French registration, not the Gabon registration of TR-. (*S.G.W.*)

Right: Over the years the same airline name crops up in different countries. Not to be confused with the Italian SE210 operator is American carrier **Altair Airlines** of Philadelphia. Beech Queenair A65 N767A is seen on the move at Washington National in July 1970. (*S.G.W.*)

Left: Pictured at Southend, U.K., in April 1987 was this **Alkair Flight Operations** Fokker F27-600 Friendship OY-APE (c/n 10443). Alkair is a Danish airline based at Copenhagen–Kastrup. (*S.G.W.*)

Above: Portuguese operator **SATA-Air Acores** Boeing 737-3Q8 CS-TGP (c/n 24131) departs Manchester–Ringway in October 1996 on a holiday charter flight. (*P.E.P.*)

Below: Avianova is part of the Alitalia group, hence the colour scheme. Operating a service to Zürich in April 1996 was this Fokker 70 I-REJO (c/n 11570). The carrier now flies as Alitalia Team. (*P.E.P.*)

Below: Based in Kiev, Ukraine, is **Air Service Ukraine**, a freight carrier. One of its fleet of Ilyushin IL-76MDs, UR-78774 (c/n 0083488643) awaits the next load of cargo at Ostend, Belgium, in May 1995. (*P.E.P.*)

Above: AMC (Aircraft Maintenance Company) is an Egyptian airline with two aircraft. Boeing 737-46B SU-SAA (c/n 24124) is photographed on the move at Zürich, April 1996. (*P.E.P.*)

Above: An airliner with 'AA' on the fin is usually owned by the mega American Airlines. Not this one, however; it is **Air Atlantique**, one of several airlines of that name, all different. It is a French operator based on the Atlantic coast at La Rochelle. F-GIIA Aérospatiale ATR 42-300 (c/n 18) arrives at Paris–Orly in June 1995. (*P.E.P.*)

Below: A wonderful colour scheme for a newly independent country. From the capital city of Yerevan comes **Armenian Airlines** Tupolev TU-154B-2 EK-85536 (c/n 536). It is at Amsterdam–Schiphol in August 1995. (*P.E.P.*)

Above: The sole long-haul aircraft operated by **Air Madagascar** is this Boeing 747-2B2B 5R-MFT (c/n 21614). It is seen at Paris–Charles de Gaulle, June 1995. (*P.E.P.*)

Above: Asiana Airlines of Seoul, Korea, has cargo services run by **Asiana Cargo**. Boeing 747-48EF HL7420 (c/n 25783) is seen on the runway at Amsterdam–Schiphol in August 1995. (*P.E.P.*)

Left: With the reunification of Germany, Berlin may now be served by a German airline. Prior to 1989 west Berlin was served by airlines from other countries. Leaping into this gap has come Tegel-based **Air Berlin**. Seen at Düsseldorf in May 1995 was this Boeing 737-4YO D-ABAD (c/n 25178). (*P.E.P.*)

Above: Starting operations in 1972 Alidair ran non-schedule operations such as newspaper cargo flights, oil industry support and holiday passenger charters. With the titles of **Alidair Scotland**, Vickers Viscount 708 G-ARIR (c/n 36) sits at Manchester–Ringway in March 1981. By 1982 the airline was operating under the name Inter City Airlines. (*P.E.P.*)

Below: Air Freight NZ is a cargo operator based in the New Zealand city of Auckland. A fleet of four Convairs is flown; seen at base in April 1992 is ZK-FTA Convair CV-580 (c/n 168). The CV-580 is a turboprop conversion of the piston-powered CV-340/-440 having a pair of Allison 501s with a power output of 3,800 shaft horsepower. (*R.O'B.*)

Above: In an area as remote as Canada's Yukon Territory an air service is more than a convenience, it is a lifeline bringing every type of goods to distant settlements. From its Whitehorse base **Air North** operates this Douglas DC-3C Dakota C-GZOF (c/n 20833). It sits with cargo door open at Vancouver in September 1992. (*R.O'B.*)

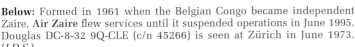

Below: Formed in 1961 when the Belgian Congo became independent Zaire, **Air Zaire** flew services until it suspended operations in June 1995. Douglas DC-8-32 9Q-CLE (c/n 45266) is seen at Zürich in June 1973. (*J.D.S.*)

Above: **Air Niugini** is the flag carrier for Papua New Guinea and is based in the capital city of Port Moresby. Photographed on a service to Brisbane, Australia, in November 1976 was Boeing 720-023 P2-ANG (c/n 18014). (*R.O'B.*)

Below: The choice of what type with which to illustrate **Air France** was made by the fact that it is, with British Airways, the only operator of supersonic transports (SST). BAe/Aérospatiale Concorde 101 F-BVFA (c/n 205) is seen arriving at Manchester–Ringway in April 1989. (*P.E.P.*)

Right: Amberair was set up in April 1988 to operate I/T and ad hoc charters. The sole fleet was this leased Boeing 737-2Q8 G-BKMS (c/n 22453) seen at Manchester–Ringway in May of that year. October of the same year saw this short-lived carrier merged into Paramount. (*P.E.P.*)

Above: The Pacific-located Republic of Nauru has an odd mix of alphabetical and numerical characters in its registration letters. C2-RN3 Boeing 737-2L7C (c/n 21073) of the national, and only, airline Air Nauru awaits passengers for a flight back home at Melbourne–Tullamarine in March 1985. (*R.O'B.*)

Above: APSA – Aerolineas Peruanas SA – was a scheduled passenger carrier based in the Peruvian capital of Lima. Arriving at London–Gatwick in August 1969 is Douglas DC-8-52 OB-R-931 (c/n 45619). (*S.G.W.*)

Below: Now over thirty-five years old, Irish cargo operator Aer Turas used to fly this Douglas C-54E Skymaster EI-ARS (c/n 27289). It is seen about to depart Liverpool–Speke on a wet April day in 1972. (*S.G.W.*)

Above: With a fleet of three passenger Boeing 707s African Airlines International operates from Nairobi in Kenya. 5Y-AXI Boeing 707-330B (c/n 18927) is seen on the ramp at base in October 1995. (*R.O'B.*)

Above: One of the great names of American domestic operators was Allegheny. Douglas DC-9-31 N985VJ (c/n 47208) is seen at New York–La Guardia in July 1970. The airline had a name change at the end of that decade to become USAir. (*S.G.W.*)

Below: Out on the ramp at the national capital, Gaborone, is Aérospatiale ATR 42-320 A2-ABC (c/n 111) of Air Botswana, March 1992. (*R.O'B.*)

Below: Korea's second airline is Asiana. Boeing 737-4Y0 HL7259 (c/n 24494) is at Fukuoka, Japan, on a service in May 1992. (*R.O'B.*)

Below: **American Flyers Airline** operated the Electra from 1963 to 1971. N125US Lockheed L-188C Electra (c/n 1101) is seen at Cleveland, Ohio, in August 1970. (*S.G.W.*)

Above: Yet another **Air Atlantique**. This one is the U.K.'s premier propliner operator based at Coventry. Seen at base in May 1989 is Douglas DC-6A G-APSA (c/n 45497). This aircraft and its sister DC-6 have now been repainted as Atlantic Cargo.

Below: Still on the books of **Air Haiti** is Curtiss C-46A Commando HH-AHA (c/n 26496) photographed at Miami in March 1981. Air Haiti is one of a long list of airlines now barred from flying into the U.S.A. because of worries about safety standards. (*R.O'B.*)

Above: New York-based **Atlas Air Cargo** has a fleet of some twenty-four cargo jumbo jets. Seen on that most spectacular of approaches, that of Hong Kong, is N507MC Boeing 747-230B (c/n 21380), February 1996. (*J.D.S.*)

Right: The name of **Air America** will for many people always be associated with the CIA operation in south-east Asia during the 1960s. Hollywood even made a film called *Air America*. Illustrated is a different Air America, a Los Angeles company founded in 1984. N303EA Lockheed L-1011 TriStar 1 (c/n 1004) is seen at Manchester–Ringway in September 1989. (*J.D.S.*)

Below: **Ansett Airlines** of Australia was one of the first operators of passenger Electras in February 1959. This Ansett Cargo Lockheed L-188AF VH-RMG (c/n 1123) was purchased in 1974 already converted for freight. It is seen at Brisbane in November 1976. (*R.O'B.*)

Below: Swiss operator **Air Engiadina**, the Swiss Regional Airline, flies an international service into London City airport, located in the heart of the business district. HB-AEF Dornier DO 328-110 (c/n 3017) lands, June 1996. (*J.D.S.*)

Right: Operating from Kazan in the autonomous Russian republic of Tartarstan is **Airstan**. The paint scheme is basic Aeroflot with just the name changed. RA76369 Ilyushin IL-76TD (c/n 1033414480) is seen at Stansted, U.K., May 1995. (*S.G.W.*)

Above: **Burrard Air** of Vancouver, British Columbia, operated an assortment of both wheel- and float-equipped aircraft on ad hoc charter work. De Havilland (Canada) DHC3 Otter C-FBCG (c/n 408) is seen at Vancouver airport sea plane base (S.P.B.) in September 1984. The airline suspended services in December 1990.

Below: The oil and gas rigs around the coast of the U.K. provide lots of helicopter support work. **Bond Helicopters** have a base at Liverpool–Speke to support Irish Sea operations. G-BLEY Eurocopter SA365N Dauphin 2 (c/n 6119) sits with the engine running as it awaits the next load of passengers in May 1995.

Above: **British Island Airways** evolved from British United. The locations served were the Channel Islands and the Isle of Man, hence the island in the name. Handley Page HPR7 Herald 213 G-AYMG (c/n 179) is seen on the move at London–Heathrow in March 1973. The company ceased operations in 1990. (*S.G.W.*)

Above: **Ansett Australia** is second in size to Qantas in the country. VH-RMO Boeing 767-204 (c/n 23807) is at Melbourne–Tullimarine in October 1996, in the company's current livery (compare with the cargo Electra). (*R.O'B.*)

Below: **Busy Bee** of Norway had bases at both Oslo and Stavanger. It was a commuter line flying scheduled passenger services. LN-NPI Fokker F27-100 Friendship (c/n 10266) is at Manchester–Ringway in May 1989. The carrier ceased operations in December 1992.

Below: German holiday charter airline **Bavaria** had this aircraft new from the manufacturer. Seen on a very wet Cologne ramp in July 1970 is BAC 111-414 D-AILY (c/n 163).

Left: Business Air of Aberdeen flies domestic services in the U.K. Short SD360 G-OJSY (c/n SH3603) is on the ramp at Liverpool–Speke, May 1989.

Below: Operating flights from Latvia to London–Gatwick in March of 1995 was this **Baltic International** Boeing 727-23 YL-BAF (c/n 18440). In November of that year the company suspended operations and regrouped to become Air Baltic.

Above: **British Asia Airways** is a subsidiary of British Airways. It was formed to operate services to Taiwan. Note the colours are basic BA with revised tail marks. G-CIVA Boeing 747-436 (c/n 27092) approaches to land on runway 27R at London–Heathrow, July 1995.

Above: With the break-up of the Soviet Union the pre-World War Two independent Baltic republics were able to regain their status as free countries. In the Latvian capital of Riga YL-LAI Tupolev TU-154M (c/n 895) of **Baltic Express Line** taxies to depart, May 1995. (*J.D.S.*)

Left: **Biman Bangladesh Airlines** is the national and only airline in Bangladesh. S2-ADB Douglas DC-10-30 (c/n 47818) is about to land at London–Heathrow in June 1996.

Below: Operating from a base at Chandler Memorial, Arizona, **Biegert Aviation** operates a fleet of seven DC-4s for freight or spray operations. N44912 Douglas DC-4 Skymaster (c/n 27231) is parked at base in October 1984. Note the spray bars on the trailing edge of the wing.

Below: **Bristow Helicopters** of the U.K. operates a worldwide support service to the offshore oil and gas industries. Seen at Aberdeen–Dyce in September 1977, from where the company services the North Sea oil platforms, is G-BBHN Sikorsky S61N (c/n 61-714).

Right: Braathens SAFE (South American and Far East) is, and has been since it was founded in 1946, a leading Norwegian charter and scheduled airline. LN-SUO Fokker F28 Fellowship (c/n 11013) is seen on the manufacturer's ramp at Amsterdam–Schiphol in July 1970. The company did not operate the F28 for many years before selling them back to Fokker. (See Special Colour Schemes, p. 143.)

Above: Balkan Bulgarian Airlines is that nation's flag carrier operating from the capital, Sofia. LZ-BTG Tupolev TU-154B (c/n 095) approaches London–Heathrow in July 1995. In more recent times western-built equipment is likely to be seen as Airbus and Boeing aircraft join the fleet.

Below: BSF – Berliner Spezialflug AG – from Berlin–Schönefeld (formerly east Berlin) operates this Beech 1900D D-CBSF (c/n UE-8), a type that seems to have lots of add-on 'bits' to wingtips and tail. Photographed at Cologne, April 1996. (*J.D.S.*)

Above: Belavia is the largest airline in the ex-Soviet republic of Belarus. Seen on a flight from the capital Minsk to Riga in May 1995 is Yakovlev YAK-40 EW83187 (c/n 9620748). There are moves within the political leadership to rejoin Russia, so the registration letters 'EW' may have a short life. (*J.D.S.*)

Above: British Midland Airways are the U.K.'s leading independent scheduled passenger carrier with both European and domestic flights. G-BVTE Fokker 70 (c/n 11538) arrives at London–Heathrow in June 1996.

Below: This Short SD330 G-EASI (c/n SH3070) is marked for **British Caledonian Commuter** as well as Genair of Liverpool. It is about to depart Liverpool–Speke in April 1983.

Below: Braniff are one of the great names in the U.S. airline world. Based in Dallas, Texas, they seem to have ceased operations and made more comebacks than Frank Sinatra, each return heralding a new livery. N465BN Boeing 727-227 (c/n 21492) is about to depart Miami, October 1981.

Above: British United Island Airways was formed from BUA to cover services to the Channel Islands and the Isle of Man. The basic BUA colours were retained. Douglas DC-3 Dakota G-AMHJ (c/n 13468), in freight mode, is seen at London–Gatwick in July 1970. People visiting Gatwick today will note that it is slightly more built up. BUIA evolved into BIA.

Above: Bar Harbor Airlines was an American east-coast commuter operator. Convair CV-600 N94208 (c/n 15) is seen on the move at Boston in August 1986. The CV-600 is a turboprop conversion of a piston-powered CV-240, with two Rolls-Royce Dart 542 engines fitted. In January 1991 the company suspended operations.

Below: Belair – Belarussian Airlines – operates both passenger and cargo flights. Out on the ramp at the carrier's base at Minsk is Ilyushin IL-76TD EW76837 (c/n 1023409316) in May 1995. (*J.D.S.*)

Below: Early in 1980 **Belize Airways Ltd**, of central America, ceased operations. The fleet was by this time in store at Miami. First in a line of five Boeing 720-022s is VP-HCP (c/n 17917), photographed in October 1981. They were all scrapped within a few years.

Below: British Mediterranean Airways has a small fleet for the one area of the world it covers, the east end of the Mediterranean. Cities covered include Beirut, Damascus and Amman. Airbus A320-231 G-MEDA (c/n 480) is seen landing at London–Heathrow, the company base, in July 1995.

Above: From the Czech Republic comes **Bemoair Praha**. The long-haul/large-capacity fleet consists of two Ilyushin IL-62Ms. OK-JBJ (c/n 4933456) is seen at Manchester–Ringway in June 1996 on a charter with football fans following the national team.

Above: Big Sky Airlines in big sky country. N5473M Swearingen SA226TC Metro II (c/n TC-281) is on the move at the company base at Billings, Montana, in August 1986. Note that on the nose it carries the logo of Northwest Airlink, to which it feeds passengers.

41

Right: BAF – British Air Ferries – was part of the same holding company as British United but run as a separate unit. It flew cars and their passengers as well as general cargo. Seen with all four Pratt & Whitney R2000 radial piston engines pounding is Aviation Traders ALT 98 Carvair G-AOFW (c/n 10351/12) at Southend, May 1972.

Above: Early in 1993 **British World Airlines** came into being with a name change from British Air Ferries. Most services are now passenger with only a few freight aircraft on the fleet. Showing off the new attractive colours at Manchester–Ringway in March 1994 is BAe 146-300 G-BRAD (c/n E3131).

Below: British Airways Express is an operation where airlines, in this case Manx, run a franchise or partnership agreement. The flights are then run as BA with aircraft in BA colours, crews in BA uniforms and BA flight numbers. BAe 4102 Jetstream 41 G-MAJE (c/n 41007) waits at Manchester–Ringway in June 1996.

Above: In what is now a constant parade of new Russian airlines this Tupolev TU-154M RA85816 (c/n 1006) belongs to **Bashkirian Airlines**. It is based at Ufa in the autonomous republic of Bashkortostan. It is photographed landing at Dubai, U.A.E., March 1997.

Above: BSL Airline of Kiev in the Ukraine operates a fleet of eleven aircraft, only one of which is not a freighter. UR76689 Ilyushin IL-78 (c/n 0063469006) is loading cargo at Sharjah, U.A.E., in March 1997. The IL-78 was built as the flying tanker version of the IL-76.

Below: Two of Switzerland's charter operators, Balair and CTA, merged in 1993 to form **Balair CTA**. Since they were owned by Swissair, in October 1995 they were merged into that company. Still in Balair CTA markings HB-INB McDonnell Douglas MD-81 (c/n 49101) operates a scheduled Swissair flight from Manchester–Ringway in June 1996. Note the distinctive yellow wings.

Below: It claims to be the world's favourite airline. It certainly operates the most photogenic aircraft. Seen arriving at the International Air Tattoo at Fairford, U.K., in July 1995 after a supersonic 'jolly' is **British Airways** BAe/Aérospatiale Concorde 102 G-BOAF (c/n 216). BA is the result of a forced merger of the two government-owned airlines BEA and BOAC. The airline was later privatised.

Below: Based at Moscow's Bykovo airport is **Bykovo Avia**, operators of this Yakovlev YAK-42 RA42322 (c/n 4520423402108). It is seen at base in August 1995.

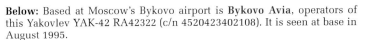

Above: BEA – British European Airways – was the state-owned flag carrier operating domestic and European scheduled flights. De Havilland (HS) 121 Trident 1E-140 G-AVYE (c/n 2139) is seen in late BEA colours at Palma, Majorca, in November 1973. This aeroplane has been preserved by the Science Museum and is in store at Wroughton, U.K.

Below: British Airways Regional was established in April 1992 and operates domestic and international scheduled services from three regional airports: Manchester, Glasgow and Birmingham. G-BGDT Boeing 737-236 (c/n 21807) is marked BA Manchester where it was seen in March 1995.

Above: British Airtours can trace its history to 1969 when it started life as BEA Airtours. The BEA/BOAC merger to form BA resulted in the new name. The task was to fly holiday charters. Seen arriving at Manchester–Ringway in September 1984 is G-BDXL Boeing 747-236B (c/n 22305) for a flight to Los Angeles in an all-economy-seat configuration. In April 1988, following the BA take-over of British Caledonian, the company was renamed Caledonian as this carrier had a good and loyal brand image.

Below: BOAC – British Overseas Airways Corporation – was the state flag carrier for long-haul scheduled services. BOAC had the honour of operating the world's first passenger jet service in May 1952 with a service to Johannesburg in South Africa with a Comet 1. This de Havilland DH106 Comet 4C N888WA (c/n 6424), however, never served with BOAC or any British operator. After service in Mexico it found its way to the U.S.A. and its eventual resting place of Everett, Washington. In 1984 it was being used by a technical school in a poor external state. The following year Boeing – who built the Comet's rival, the 707 – repainted the aircraft to the current markings. Pictured August 1986.

Above: B Airways of Miami must have the shortest name for an airline. N2685W Douglas DC-3 Dakota (c/n 33010) approaches to land on runway 9L at base, June 1989. The following year the company suspended operations.

Above: BUA – British United Airways – was formed in 1960 with the merger of no fewer than eight airlines. The operator was launch customer for the BAC 111. G-AWYV model 501 (c/n 178) is at home base of London–Gatwick in May 1970. At the end of that year the carrier was purchased by Caledonian to form British Caledonian.

Right: Buffalo Airways is an American freight operator based in Kansas City, Missouri. N161DB Douglas DC-8-61F (c/n 45980) departs London–Gatwick in August 1993. It is of note that the company name is carried only in the logo on the fin and does not appear on the cabin roof.

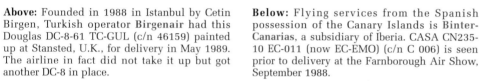

Above: Founded in 1988 in Istanbul by Cetin Birgen, Turkish operator **Birgenair** had this Douglas DC-8-61 TC-GUL (c/n 46159) painted up at Stansted, U.K., for delivery in May 1989. The airline in fact did not take it up but got another DC-8 in place.

Below: Flying services from the Spanish possession of the Canary Islands is **Binter-Canarias**, a subsidiary of Iberia. CASA CN235-10 EC-011 (now EC-EMO) (c/n C 006) is seen prior to delivery at the Farnborough Air Show, September 1988.

Above: Brit'air of France this time. The company flies services around that country from Morlaix. It also flies to the U.K. where F-GHMJ Saab 340A (c/n 340A-136) is seen about to land at London–Gatwick in August 1993.

Above: American commuter operator **Britt Airways** got its name from the founder Mr Britt. N325BA Swearingen SA226TC Metro II (c/n TC-304), with its Garrett TPE 331 turboprops running, departs Dayton, Ohio, in July 1986. The company, like most commuters, took on a partnership with a large carrier, in this case Continental Express.

Below: Canadian backwoods operators have to be able to go any place and carry anything. Such a company is **Bradley Air Services Ltd**. Douglas DC-3 Dakota C-FQNF (c/n 26643) is seen at Oshawa, Ontario, in July 1986.

Below: BASE (Business Aviation Services Eindhoven) is a small Dutch operator with a fleet of three BAe 3018 Jetstream 31s. PH-KJA (c/n 645) is seen on a charter to an airshow at Boscombe Down, U.K., in June 1992.

Above: Bridgeport, Connecticut, airline **Business Express** now flies under the banner of the Delta Connection. Seen prior to that in May 1989 at Washington National is Saab SF340A N344BE (c/n 340A-104).

Above: U.S. freight operator **Burlington Air Express** of Toledo, Ohio, was flying this Boeing 707-321C N863BX (c/n 19270) from Miami in June 1989.

Right: **Bearskin Airlines** of Sioux Lookout, Ontario, operates a growing fleet of commuter aircraft in the north of the Canadian province. Beechcraft B99 Airliner C-GFQC (c/n U120) formats with a camera ship, a Bearskin Piper T1040, on a flight from Pickle Lake to the company base in June 1990.

Below: **Birmingham Executive Airways** is one of the only U.K. operators to fly services in Grumman G159 Gulfstream 1s. G-BMOW (c/n 155) is seen at base, Birmingham–Elmdon, in July 1988. Within the year the company name was changed to Birmingham European.

Below: **Birmingham European Airways** operated this Fokker 50 on lease from Maersk, hence the basic blue colour with just titles added. OY-MMV (c/n 20154) is at Birmingham–Elmdon in May 1989.

Left: The Bahamas is a bright and sunny chain of islands. **Bahamasair** reflects this in the company's bright colours. Boeing 737-2L9 C6-BEQ (c/n 21279) is seen about to depart Miami on the short flight to Nassau in June 1989.

Above: When the Berlin Wall fell in 1989 the Germans in the east wanted to travel to the sun as their western countrymen had done for many years. They were not as well off, so they flew in older propjets rather than new and shiny jets. D-AOAU Ilyushin IL-18D (c/n 188010904) of **Berline** descends over Glyfada to land on Athens runway 33R in June 1993. In October the following year it suspended operations and the fleet was sold.

Right: Bangkok Airways de Havilland (Canada) DHC8 – 8-102 HS-SKH (c/n 144) taxies into the domestic terminal at Bangkok–Don Muang International, November 1989.

Above: British Caledonian Airways used to be the second largest U.K. airline with both domestic and long-haul international services. It was taken over by British Airways in 1988. G-BHDJ Douglas DC10-30 (c/n 47840) lands on runway 25L at Los Angeles–LAX in September 1988.

Below: BWIA International of Trinidad and Tobago used to be known as British West Indian Airways. From the base in Port of Spain it operates services around the Caribbean and further afield. Lockheed L-1011 TriStar 500 9Y-TGN (c/n 1191) is on approach to London–Heathrow in September 1993.

Above: Britannia Airways are one of the U.K.'s largest holiday charter operators flying a fleet of Boeing 757/767 to destinations as far away as Australia. G-BRIG Boeing 767-204 (c/n 24757) is about to touch down on runway 06 at Manchester–Ringway in April 1991.

Right: Blue Scandinavia is the new name for Transwede Leisure. It was adopted in October 1996. The Swedish holiday charter operator brought this Boeing 757-2YO SE-DUL (c/n 26151) into Sharjah, U.A.E., in March 1997 to refuel on its way to Phuket in Thailand.

Below: Balair was a leading Swiss charter airline, owned by Swissair, flying from its base at Zürich. Following a merger with CTA they were absorbed into Swissair. Fokker F27-200 Friendship HB-AAV (c/n 10276) is at Geneva in July 1970.

Below: U.K. carrier Brymon Airways is based in the west of England at Plymouth. Services include a schedule to London–Heathrow. G-BRYA de Havilland (Canada) DHC7 Dash 7 (c/n 62) arrives at Liverpool–Speke in June 1988. The airline now operates as a British Airways franchise company and flies in BA colours.

Below: Seen arriving at Singapore in December 1996 is PK-IJJ Boeing 737-230 (c/n 22130) of local Indonesian operator **Bouraq**. (*R.O'B.*)

Above: **Bush Pilots Airways** from Cairns, Queensland, flew both freight and passengers around the Australian bush. Douglas DC-3 Dakota VH-EDD (c/n 25367) is at Melbourne–Essendon in November 1976. Three months later the aircraft was grounded at Cairns and cannibalised for parts. (*R.O'B.*)

Below: **Bulair** (the title on the cabin roof is in Cyrillic script) was a state-run airline affiliated to Balkan Bulgarian, based in the capital, Sofia. LZ-BEL Ilyushin IL-18V (c/n 4601) is at London–Gatwick in September 1968. By 1973 the fleet of IL-18/AN-12/AN-24s had been transferred over to Balkan. (*S.G.W.*)

Above: **BBA Cargo** (Brain and Brown Airfreighters) was based at Melbourne–Essendon. VH-BAB Douglas DC-3 Dakota (c/n 25495) is at base in December 1979. The company had just ceased trading when the photograph was taken. (*R.O'B.*)

Above: **Cubana** is Cuba's national airline. Seen on a scheduled passenger flight at Santo Domingo, Dominican Republic, is Yakovlev YAK-42D CU-T1277 (c/n 4520423016238).

Below: **Contract Air Cargo** of Pontiac, Michigan, operates what must be the smartest Skymaster in the world. N4989K Douglas C-54 (c/n 27319) is at Borinquen, Puerto Rico, in November 1992.

Above: **CF Air Freight** (Consolidated Freightways) is an American parcel carrier. In 1989 it took over Emery and now operates in that company's livery. N991CF Douglas DC-8F-54 (c/n 45801) is arriving at San Diego in September 1988.

Above: **CAVE** (Compania Aerea de Viajes Expressos) was a Venezuelan commuter operator. Formed in 1987, it suspended services in 1993. Seen from the observation deck on the domestic terminal at Caracas–Maiquetia/Simon Bolivar in November 1992 is YV-472C Swearingen SA226TC Metro II (c/n TC-262).

Right: City Express was a Canadian commuter airline based at Toronto Island Airport. Seen on a service to Hamilton, Ontario, in July 1986 is C-FFZP Saunders ST27 (c/n 010/14070). The ST27 is a conversion of the de Havilland DH114 Heron in which the four Gipsy Queen inline piston engines are replaced by two PT6A turboprops of 715shp. Other modifications included an increase in the fuselage length, a re-engineered wing, and a nose extended to take a radar set. A total of twelve ST27s were converted by this Canadian company. As for City Express, it ceased operations in February 1991.

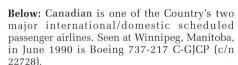

Above: Seen at Medellin, Colombia, engineless, in November 1992 is Douglas DC-3 Dakota HK3199 (c/n 26044) of **Costa Colombia** (Compania Sinuana de Transporte Aereo Costa). In 1994 the airline suspended services.

Below: Canadian is one of the Country's two major international/domestic scheduled passenger airlines. Seen at Winnipeg, Manitoba, in June 1990 is Boeing 737-217 C-GJCP (c/n 22728).

Above: Coral Colombia is a small freight operator based at Villavicencio. Seen on the runway at base, November 1992, is that great propliner cargo aircraft the Curtiss C-46A Commando HK851 (c/n 383).

Above: CAAC (Civil Aviation Administration of China) used to be the sole operating airline in that country, just as Aeroflot was in the U.S.S.R. In the mid-1980s the government gave independence to the regions to operate as self-managed units. Still as CAAC at London–Gatwick is Boeing 747-2J6B B2448 (c/n 23461). In July 1986.

Below: Flying meat into La Paz, Bolivia, with a fleet of just this one aircraft was **CAN** – Compania Aerea Nacional. Douglas DC-6 CP1654 (c/n 43035) is seen at the end of a meat run in November 1992. Note, being poured out of the cargo door, the blood and offal waste as the interior is hosed out! The airline lost its aircraft in March 1993 and has not replaced it.

Below: Carnival Air Lines of Fort Lauderdale, Florida, operates by flying passengers to and from cruise ships; scheduled services are also flown. It operates Boeing 737-212 N161FN (c/n 20521), seen about to depart San Juan, Puerto Rico, in November 1992.

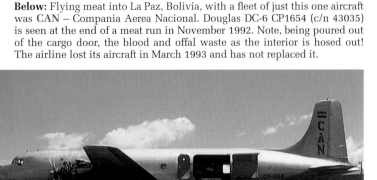

Below: Seen parked at Seattle–Tacoma in August 1986 is **Cascade Airways** BAC 111-401PK N217CA (c/n 63). Exactly one year earlier the carrier had filed for Chapter 11 of the U.S. Bankruptcy Laws. Despite an intention to restart, it did not.

Below: The whole fleet of **Caicos Caribbean Airways** is pictured at Fort Lauderdale in May 1989. N34867 Douglas DC-6A (c/n 44624). In a freight configuration it plies its trade to the Turks and Caicos Islands, a U.K. colony in the Caribbean.

Above: **Cal Air** was another of the companies to emerge from the BCAL/BA merger. They used to be British Caledonian Airways (Charter) Ltd. G-BJZD Douglas DC-10-10 (c/n 46970) is on push-back at Manchester–Ringway in June 1988.

Below: One of the many DC-3 operators to be found at Villavicencio, Colombia, is **Calamar**. The company does not, as can be seen, go in for flash colour schemes. HK3462X Douglas DC-3 Dakota (c/n 11759) is at base in November 1992.

Below: The perfect aircraft for the location but it sits damaged and out of service. HK1241 Britten-Norman BN2A Islander (c/n 265) is in the colours of **Caribena** at Villavicencio, Colombia, in November 1992.

Right: British domestic airline **Connectair** was based at London–Gatwick. Seen landing there in July 1988 is Short SD330-200 G-BITV (c/n SH3068). Note the effects of the engine exhaust on the fin colours. In 1989 the airline was renamed Air Europe Express.

Below: **NLM City Hopper** operates feeder services from its Amsterdam base. PH-CHD Fokker F28 Fellowship 4000 (c/n 11139) is on a charter to Liverpool–Speke in April 1983. The company is owned by KLM and now flies as KLM City Hopper.

Below: **Central Air Transport** of Ontario, Canada, operates this de Havilland (Canada) DHC3 Otter C-FGTL (c/n 10). Its function is to fly whatever and whoever will fit inside to any place with sufficient water to land on. In the long cold winters many such aircraft will swap floats for skis. The aircraft is at Pickle Lake S.P.B. in northern Ontario, June 1990.

Right: CSA (Ceskoslovenske Aerolinie) was the national airline for Czechoslovakia. With the peaceful split of the country into the Czech and the Slovak Republics it is now CSA Czech Airlines. OK-TCB Tupolev TU-154M (c/n 770) is at London–Heathrow in May 1988. Most services to Heathrow are now carried out by western-built aircraft; the Russian gas guzzlers will soon be a thing of the past.

Above: Thunder Bay is in the less populated northern part of the province of Ontario. Here is another aircraft of Ontario Express but this time marked as **Canadian Frontier**. Both colour schemes are based on the major carrier Canadian. C-GFAD Beechcraft 1900C-1 Airliner (c/n UC-83). Photograph taken June 1990.

Below: CTA (Compagnie de Transport Aérien) was a Swiss charter airline based at Geneva. HB-ICQ Sud Aviation SE210 Caravelle 10B (c/n 222) arrives at Zürich, August 1987. CTA was owned by Swissair who first merged them with Balair, and then later absorbed the new company.

Above: Flying commuters in the colours of **Canadian Partner** is this Ontario Express BAe 3112 Jetstream 31 C-GJPH (c/n 738). It is seen in the south of the province at Hamilton in June 1990.

Above: From the Greek island of Crete comes **Cretan Airlines**. Seen landing at Athens in June 1993 is Airbus A320-231 SX-BAS (c/n 043).

Below: Cyprus Airways has an all-Airbus fleet. It flies scheduled and holiday charters from its base at Larnaca. 5B-DAS Airbus A310-203 (c/n 352) is about to land at Manchester–Ringway in March 1991.

Below: Condor is a large German holiday charter airline owned by Lufthansa. The company has always had a distinctive yellow tail. D-ABNO Boeing 757-230 (c/n 25901) is on approach to Athens, June 1993.

Below: Challenge Air Cargo of Miami is one of the more 'upmarket' freight movers at that airport. The all-jet fleet includes three Boeing 757 freighters. Seen here is the classic Boeing 707-330C N707HE (c/n 20124) at base in June 1989.

Above: Swiss operator **Crossair**, based at Basle, can now be found operating scheduled passenger services around Europe. HB-IXD BAe 146-200 (c/n E2073) is seen prior to delivery at the Farnborough Air Show, September 1990. (See Special Colour Schemes, p. 141.)

Below: CityFlyer Express is a London–Gatwick-based commuter airline. G-BUEA Aérospatiale ATR 42-300 (c/n 268) arrives at base in August 1993. The airline now operates a franchise agreement with BA and flies in BA's colours.

Above: The U.K. colony of the Cayman Islands is a renowned tax haven. Operating to Georgetown on Grand Cayman from Miami is **Cayman Airways** BAC 111-531PS VR-CAB (c/n 237). It is seen at the latter location in October 1981.

Below: Canadian charter carrier **Canada 3000** used to be mistaken for the U.K. operator Air 2000 as the fleet mix and colour scheme were all but interchangeable. The companies are associated. Late in 1996 both airlines changed their livery. C-FXOF Boeing 757-28A (c/n 24544) arrives at Manchester–Ringway in June 1996 after an Atlantic crossing.

Above: Flying this superbly painted Douglas DC-6A is **Cayman Airways Cargo**. N61267 (c/n 45374) is at Miami in October 1981.

Above: French charter operator **Corsair** can be found at many worldwide holiday resorts. F-GFUH Boeing 737-4B3 (c/n 24751) arrives at Athens in June 1993.

Right: Quite simply the best way to fly is to go by flying boat. **Chalks International Airlines** flies from Florida to the Bahamas. It can lay claim to being one of the world's oldest airlines, having been founded as far back as 1919! N2442H Grumman G73 Mallard (c/n J13) arrives at Bimini in the Bahamas after a flight from Nassau in October 1981. The airline now flies under the name of Pan Am Air Bridge.

Above: Showing off the new livery of **Continental Airlines**, one of the largest scheduled passenger carriers in the U.S.A., is N27783 Boeing 727-232 (c/n 20638) seen at Tampa, Florida, in April 1994.

Below: **Capitol Airways** was one of the few U.S. airlines to be seen doing charter flights to Europe in the late 1960s. N4908C Douglas DC-8-63 (c/n 45968) is seen arriving on a trooping charter at Frankfurt in July 1970. The Tennessee-based carrier suspended operations in November 1984.

Above: **Cathay Pacific**, based in Hong Kong, has a history going back to 1946. It has a large fleet and flies scheduled passenger services worldwide. VR-HOZ Boeing 747-467 (c/n 25871) departs Manchester–Ringway in March 1997 in the carrier's old colours.

Above: **Caspian Airlines** are a Tehran, Iran-based carrier with a fleet of three aircraft. EP-CPE Yakovlev YAK-42D arrives at Dubai, U.A.E., in March 1997. (*J.D.S.*)

Below: Flying feeder services for Continental is this **Continental Express** Saab SF340A N404BH (c/n 340A-061) seen at Miami in June 1989. The colour scheme for both arms of the company has since been changed.

Below: Irish independent **Cityjet** flies this BAe 146-200A EI-JET (c/n E2073) on services. It is seen arriving at Manchester–Ringway in June 1996.

Above: Croatia is one of the ex-Yugoslavia countries. From Zagreb comes **Croatia Airlines** Boeing 737-230 9A-CTE (c/n 22634) to London–Heathrow in July 1995.

Below: Canadian Pacific is a great name in transport, not just air travel; the train service is even immortalised in song. C-GCPO Boeing 737-217 (c/n 21718) is at Toronto in July 1986. In April the following year the carrier merged with Pacific Western to form Canadian. (See Special Colour Schemes, p. 143.)

Above: Based in the Latvian capital of Riga, **Concors** – Latvian Air Service operates this single Czech-built LET 410UVP-E YL-KAC (c/n 851531). It is seen in the static exhibition of the Russian trade air show at Zhukovsky, August 1995.

Below: Flying services from Panama City is **COPA Panama** (Compania Panamena de Aviación) Boeing 737-204 HP-1163-CMP (c/n 21693). It is seen on runway 9L at Miami in April 1994. Note the long registration.

Below: Short-lived British independent airline was **Community Express**. Seen at Liverpool–Speke was this BAe 3012 Jetstream 31 G-BRGN (c/n 637), it used to operate a scheduled service to London–Gatwick. It was photographed in August 1996 shortly before the carrier suspended operations.

Above: Flying holiday charters from the Spanish island of Majorca was **Centennial**. McDonnell Douglas MD-83 EC-607 (now EC-FVV) (c/n 49708) arrives at Manchester–Ringway in March 1994. In October 1996 flying ceased and the aircraft was repossessed.

Above: Seen arriving at Manchester–Ringway in June 1996 full of football fans is Belgian charter airline **ChallengAir** Douglas DC-10-30 OO-JOT (c/n 46850). Note it also has the name of French operator Corsair on the cabin roof; this is due to a sub-lease.

Right: American commuter operator **ComAir** is seen flying Brazilian-built Embraer 110P1 Bandeirante N64CZ (c/n 110399) from Miami in June 1989. The airline flies as a feeder for Delta.

Above: Channel Airways was a British independent which took that name in 1956. Both holiday charter as well as scheduled services were flown from the company base at Southend. G-AVNJ Vickers Viscount 812 (c/n 361) is at base in May 1972. The company suspended services in February of that year.

Above: LAC – Lineas Aereas Canarias – was a Spanish airline based in Tenerife. EC-EMG McDonnell Douglas MD-83 (c/n 49626) is at East Midlands–Castle Donington in August 1989. The airline merged into Meridiana Air in 1990. (P.E.P.)

Below: Caicos International Limited flew this Douglas C-54D Skymaster N122AC (c/n 10748) from 1973 to 1975. It is seen on the ramp at Fort Lauderdale in July 1974. (S.G.W.)

Above: Now owned by a holiday company, **Caledonian Airways** has gone through a number of owners and name variations. Lockheed L-1011 TriStar 100 G-BBAJ (c/n 1106) is pushed back from Manchester–Ringway Terminal 1 in March 1995.

Above: Danish operator **Cimber Air** flies from Soenderborg. Seen on a service to Frankfurt in April 1996 is Aérospatiale ATR 42-300 OY-CIG (c/n 019). (J.D.S.)

Below: Following the mid-1980s split of CAAC came a spate of regional Chinese airlines. Airbus A310-222 B2301 (c/n 311) of **China Northwest**, based in Xian, lands at Hong Kong in February 1996. (J.D.S.)

Below: Casair – Caribbean Air Services – operated this Curtiss C-46 Commando on cargo services. N4803J (c/n 30386) is seen at El Paso, Texas, in October 1984. By early 1985 the company had suspended operations and this aeroplane was sold to Air Manitoba.

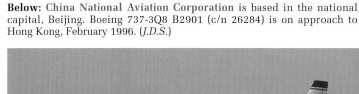

Below: China National Aviation Corporation is based in the national capital, Beijing. Boeing 737-3Q8 B2901 (c/n 26284) is on approach to Hong Kong, February 1996. (*J.D.S.*)

Above: From the city of Chengdu comes **China Southern**. Boeing 737-5Y0 B2550 (c/n 25188) is seen at Hong Kong in February 1996. (*J.D.S.*)

Below: Operating **China Airlines Cargo** is this Boeing 747-209F B160 (c/n 24308) at Anchorage, Alaska, in July 1991. (*R.O'B.*)

Above: China Eastern is based in the port city of Shanghai. McDonnell Douglas MD-11 B2175 (c/n 48520) arrives at Hong Kong, February 1996. (*J.D.S.*)

Below: The 'other' China is Taiwan. It is of note that two countries with different governments, outlooks and claims over each other have the same registration letter. B1802 Airbus A300-622R (c/n 533) of **China Airlines**, Taipei, is photographed at Hong Kong in February 1996. (*J.D.S.*)

Above: Cargo Lion is a freight operator flying DC-8s, based in Ostend, Belgium, but flying Luxembourg-registered aircraft. LX-TLB Douglas DC-8-62F (c/n 45925) is seen about to depart Sharjah, U.A.E., in March 1997.

Above: Cargolux is Luxembourg's largest freight mover with a fleet of eight Jumbos. LX-GCV Boeing 747-4R7F (c/n 25867) taxies to the cargo area at Manchester–Ringway in May 1996. (*P.E.P.*)

Below: Catalina Airlines used this Grumman G21A Goose N322 (c/n B73) between Long Beach and San Pedro on Catalina Island. It is seen at the former in October 1976. (*S.G.W.*)

Below: Zürich-based **Classic Air** operated two Dakotas for sightseeing and pleasure flights. HB-ISC Douglas DC-3 Dakota (c/n 9995) is at base in August 1987. In 1995 the airline suspended operations.

Above: With a fleet of just one aircraft, Bolivian cargo carrier **Compania Boliviana de Aviación** operates from Cochabamba. Douglas DC-3 Dakota CP1419 (c/n 32988) is seen at Santa Cruz–El Trompillo in November 1992.

Below: Seen at Bangkok in September 1994 is **Cambodia International Airlines** Boeing 737-2E1 N197AL (c/n 20300). Three months later the carrier suspended operations, hoping to restart with a new name. (*R.O'B.*)

Right: Starting life in Wales in 1935 **Cambrian Airways** grew to be a major British independent, flying scheduled passenger services around the U.K. In 1972 it was absorbed into British Airways. Vickers Viscount 701 G-ALWF (c/n 5) is seen at Liverpool–Speke in September 1970. This aircraft was the oldest surviving Viscount and is now preserved at Duxford. (*S.G.W.*)

Above: The CIA logo on the fin is not that of everybody's favourite spy organisation. This CIA is **Channel Islands Aviation** operating a mixed fleet of single- and twin-engined types from the company base at Camarillo, California. N55JA Britten-Norman BN2A Islander (c/n 295) is at base in September 1988.

Below: Aircraft from the Democratic People's Republic of Korea, i.e. North Korea, are very, very rare in the west. **Chosonminhang Korean Airways** Ilyushin IL-62M P885 (c/n 3933913) lands at Manchester–Ringway in July 1991 with a team of athletes for the World Student Games being held in Sheffield. The airline now uses the title Air Koryo.

Below: Chinese airline **China Northern** flies from the city of Shenyang. Like most of its sister operators it mostly flies western-built aircraft. B2134 McDonnell Douglas MD-82 (c/n 49518) lands against rain-filled clouds at Hong Kong, November 1995. (*R.O'B.*)

Below: Seen at Miami in October 1981 is this short-body Boeing 727-41 HI-212 (c/n 20426) of **Dominicana de Aviación**. Services are run from the capital of the Dominican Republic, Santo Domingo.

Above: Seen landing at Dubai, U.A.E., in March 1997 is VR-HVY Boeing 747-236F (c/n 22306) of **Cathay Pacific Cargo**. This shows off well the Hong Kong-based airline's current livery.

Below: **Desert Sun Airlines** of Long Beach, California, flew this Beechcraft 99A Airliner N51PA (c/n U-80). It is seen at Los Angeles–LAX in September 1984. During 1987 the carrier ceased operations.

Above: Flying a French-registered Airbus is **Diamond Sakha**. This Russian airline is from the autonomous republic of Sakha-Yakutia. It is another example of the very smart colours that can be seen flying around the former U.S.S.R. F-OGYN Airbus A310-324ET (c/n 458) is departing Moscow–Sheremetyevo, September 1995.

Right: At one time **Dan Air** was one of the largest independent airlines in Europe. The history goes back to 1953 and the name is derived from the shipping broker owners Davies and Newman. Boeing 737-3Q8 G-BNNJ (c/n 24068) arrives at Manchester–Ringway in March 1991. The airline was taken over by British Airways in November the following year.

Below: Seen in store in October 1984 at Pinal Air Park, Marana, Arizona, is Shorts SD360-100 N131DA (c/n SH3631) of **Dash Air**. This Santa Ana, California-based commuter airline had suspended services that year.

Below: Argentinian operator **Dinar Lineas Aereas** flies from Buenos Aires Aeroparque. In 1995 it had on lease from Aero Lloyd, Germany, this McDonnell Douglas MD-82 D-ALLT (c/n 49440). It is seen departing base in November of that year. (R.O'B.)

Right: Photographed landing at the Farnborough Air Show in September 1984 is Dornier DO228-200 D-IASX (c/n 8035) of **Delta Air**, a German commuter airline. In June 1992 the airline was renamed Deutsche BA.

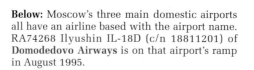

Above: DAS Air Cargo of Entebbe, Uganda, has been operating 707s to the U.K. for some years. New to the fleet is Douglas DC-10-30F 5X-JOE (c/n 47906). It is seen making a flypast at the Biggin Hill Air Show in June 1996. (*S.G.W.*)

Below: Moscow's three main domestic airports all have an airline based with the airport name. RA74268 Ilyushin IL-18D (c/n 18811201) of **Domodedovo Airways** is on that airport's ramp in August 1995.

Above: The BA in **Deutsche BA** stands for British Airways, the airline colours being quite similar to those of BA. It is all part of BA's global expansion to buy a German regional airline. D-ADBD Boeing 737-3L9 (c/n 27061) is seen at Düsseldorf, May 1995. (*P.E.P.*)

Above: DAT – Belgian Regional Airlines is a subsidiary of the national flag carrier Sabena. The DAT was derived from Delta Air Transport (Delta is a name used by a number of operators). Fokker F28-3000 Fellowship OO-DJA (c/n 11163) is about to depart Zürich, August 1987.

Below: Donaldson International Airways got its first aircraft in 1967. The carrier flew British holidaymakers to the sun. G-AOVF Bristol 175 Britannia 312 (c/n 13237) is at Coventry, U.K., in November 1972. The airline suspended operations in August 1974. This Britannia is now preserved in BOAC colours at the Royal Air Force Museum at Cosford. (*S.G.W.*)

Below: Still flying piston-engined Convairs is **Dodita Air Cargo** of San Juan, Puerto Rico. N355T Convair CV-240 (c/n 281) runs its engines at base in November 1992.

Above: This Curtiss C-46F Commando HK3079X (c/n 22538) of **Dainco** Colombia was impounded for suspected drug running at Villavicencio. It was seen in November 1992; in May 1995 it crashed into a hillside nearby.

Below: **DHL** Worldwide Express is one of the world leaders in flying small parcels and documents around the globe. Boeing 727-35F OO-DHQ (c/n 19167) is seen making a regular early morning flight into Athens in June 1993.

Below: A start-up carrier in 1996 was Dutch airline **Denim Air**. PH-DMB Fokker 50 (c/n 20264) lands at London–City, June 1996. *(J.D.S.)*

Above: American mega carrier **Delta Air Lines** of Atlanta, Georgia, operates services to a number of British airports. N762DA Lockheed L-1011 TriStar 500 (c/n 1210) lands at Manchester–Ringway in March 1994.

Above: **Debonair** is a new U.K. airline based at Luton. G-DEBA BAe 146-200 (c/n E2028) is at base, June 1996. *(J.D.S.)*

Below: Seen at Fort Lauderdale in November 1992 is this cargo Douglas DC-6 N4163Q (c/n 43681) of **Dio'air**.

Above: Hong Kong-based **Dragonair** has an all-Airbus fleet. VR-HYU Airbus A320-231 (c/n 447) is at base in February 1996. *(J.D.S.)*

Above: Founded in 1992 **Dakota National Air** operates a fleet of six passenger aircraft – Dakotas of course. VH-UPQ Douglas DC-3C (c/n 33300) is at the company base of Sydney–Bankstown in December 1996. *(R.O'B.)*

Right: Excalibur Airways was founded in 1992 and originally flew European holiday charter operations. G-HAGT Airbus A320-212 (c/n 294) lands at Manchester–Ringway in March 1993. The plan for 1996 was to fly two DC-10s on long-haul charters, the A320s having gone back to the lease company. There was a delay in getting its own DC-10 so another was leased. There was a safety scare with this that was blazed over the newspapers to such an extent that public confidence collapsed, and so, in June, did the airline.

Above: This Tajik Air Antonov AN-26B EY-26205 (c/n 14107) is on lease to **Daallo Airlines**; note the logo on the nose. This carrier is based at Djibouti in the horn of Africa. All the airline's fleet are leased from other companies. It is seen at Sharjah in March 1997.

Below: EPA (Eastern Provincial Airways) was a Canadian carrier based in Nova Scotia. C-FEPO Boeing 737-2E1 (c/n 20300) is seen at Toronto in July 1986. The following year the airline became one of the group forming Canadian.

Above: Donavia Airlines is a Russian carrier based at Rostov-na-Donu. It has a fleet of over forty aircraft. Operating one of its cargo services is Antonov AN-12B RA11115 (c/n 01348003). It is seen landing at Dubai in March 1997. (*J.D.S.*)

Above: Eastern Airlines was one of the oldest names in American flying annals since its formation in 1928. N334EA Lockheed L-1011 TriStar 1 (c/n 1141) climbs out of Miami in October 1981. The airline suspended services in January of 1991. (See Special Colour Schemes, p. 143.)

Below: Emerald Airways of Liverpool flies a mix of freight and passengers in its all-HS748 fleet. G-BGMO Avro (HS) 748-347 Srs 2A (c/n 1767) taxies to depart base in September 1996.

Below: National flag carrier for Egypt is **Egypt Air**, based in Cairo. Boeing 737-566 SU-GBL (c/n 26051) lands in evening sun at Athens, June 1993.

Above: Flying services from Addis Ababa is **Ethiopian Airlines**. Landing at London–Heathrow in July 1995 is Boeing 767-260 ET-AIE (c/n 23106).

Above: Operating from Dubai in the United Arab Emirates, located in the Persian Gulf, is the national airline **Emirates**. Boeing 777-21H A6-EME (c/n 27248) lands at London–Heathrow in July 1996.

Above: **Eastern Express** was the American commuter operator feeding the main Eastern Airlines company. Saab SF340A N404BH (c/n 340A-061) is at Boston, Massachusetts, in August 1986. As with the main company, in January 1991 the airline ceased operations.

Below: **Eva Air** of Taiwan was the first airline from that country to operate a regular service to the U.K. N405EV Boeing 747-45E (c/n 27142) is about to depart London–Gatwick in October 1993. The airline is part of the American Evergreen Group, hence the aircraft registration.

Below: Dallas, Texas-based **Express One** is an all-727 freight operator. Seen in May 1989 at a very wet Philadelphia is short-body Boeing 727-31F N220NE (c/n 18905).

Below: **Europe Aero Services** was a large operator of the Vickers V952 Vanguard. F-BVUY (c/n 744) is at Paris–Le Bourget in June 1977. Most of the Vanguard fleet was withdrawn from use at the company base at Perpignan.

Below: **EAS Europe Airlines** was the new name and livery of Europe Aero Services. Boeing 737-2A1 F-GHXK (c/n 21599) is on a service at Dublin in June 1994. In March of the following year operations were suspended.

Below: **Eagle Air Cargo** of Iceland operated this Lockheed L-188A Electra TF-VLN (c/n 1096) for only a year. The aircraft is seen at Rotterdam in June 1983.

Right: You would look long and hard to find this **Empire Airways**. It is a fictional airline created by a TV company for a series about Agatha Christie's famous Belgian detective Poirot. The aircraft is Douglas DC-3 Dakota G-AMRA (c/n 26735) owned by Air Atlantique; it is at the International Air Tattoo at Fairford in July 1991.

Above: ERA Aviation of Anchorage, Alaska, operates a large fleet of helicopters plus a smaller number of fixed-wing types. N566EA Convair CV-580 (c/n 381) is at base in July 1992. (*R.O'B.*)

Below: Exparc was another of Russia's new airlines. It operated a fleet of two Ilyushin IL-76TD cargo aircraft. RA76818 (c/n 1013408264) is at base of Moscow–Sheremetyevo in September 1995. This was the year the airline suspended operations.

Above: European Airlines was a Belgium-based charter operator. OO-MKO Airbus A300B4-103 (c/n 65) is pushed back from Terminal 2 at Manchester–Ringway in March 1994. On New Year's Day 1996 the airline suspended operations.

Above: EBA – EuroBelgian Airlines – is an all-737 operator with services to many locations around Europe. OO-LTO Boeing 737-33A (c/n 25011) is landing at Athens in June 1993. In 1996 the company was bought by the Virgin Group.

Below: Emery Worldwide is one of the big U.S. parcel/document movers. Boeing 727-51C N415EX (c/n 18945) is parked up for the day at Omaha, Nebraska, in July 1986.

Below: Bulgarian carrier **European Airlines** owns this Ilyushin IL-18D LZ-AZO (c/n 184007405). It is seen on the ramp at Sharjah, U.A.E., in March 1997.

Above: British Independent **Eurodirect** came and went in a year. G-OEDH BAe ATP (c/n 2039) shows off the attractive colours of the airline at London–Gatwick in September 1994. The carrier suspended services in February 1995. (*J.D.S.*)

Below: Late in 1996 **Ecuatoriana** was reborn with a new owner, VASP of Brazil. HC-BVM Boeing 727-2M7 (c/n 21502) is being prepared for delivery at Tucson in October 1996. Note the similarity with the VASP livery. (*J.D.S.*)

Below: European Aircharter – EAC – has cornered the market in BAC 111 ad hoc operations and charters. G-AVMI BAC 111-510ED (c/n 137) lines up to depart Dublin, June 1994.

Above: **Ecuatoriana** of Quito in Ecuador had a most colourful livery. HC-BFC Boeing 707-321B (c/n 19277) is about to depart Miami in June 1989. Operations were suspended in September 1993.

Right: Portuguese operator **Eurafric** bought this Bristol 175 Britannia 235 EI-BCI (c/n 13449) to run services between Lisbon and Luanda in Angola. It is seen here at Luton, U.K., in May 1978. The aircraft was delivered to Lisbon but no revenue flights were made and it did not take up a Portuguese registration. It was in fact then used by Irish operator Aer Turas on lease. (*J.D.S.*)

Left: **El Dorado** – Colombia is one of many Dakota operators based at Villavicencio. HK2666 Douglas DC-3 (c/n 10201) is at base in November 1992.

Above: German scheduled passenger airline **Eurowings** is based in Nuremburg. Aérospatiale ATR 42-300 D-BDDD (c/n 110) lands at London–Gatwick in August 1993.

Right: **East African Airways** was founded in 1946 to cover British colonial territory. Kenya, Tanzania and Uganda all formed national airlines in the years following independence. Vickers (BAC) Super VC10 1154 5X-UVA (c/n 881) is at London–Heathrow in August 1970. This aircraft was destroyed by fire following a take-off abort at Addis Ababa in April 1972. (S.G.W.)

Above: National airline of Israel is **El Al**; it operates from Tel Aviv. 4X-EBR Boeing 757-258 (c/n 24254) arrives at Manchester–Ringway in April 1991. The carrier is well known for having the toughest security of any airline.

Below: The Baltic republic of Estonia is one of the three re-independent countries following the collapse of the U.S.S.R. ES-AAS Yakovlev YAK-40 (c/n 9632049) is operated by **Estonian Air** from the carrier's base at Tallinn. It was photographed there in May 1995. (J.D.S.)

Above: **Evergreen International** operates services for all aspects of aviation. Lockheed L-188 Electra N5534 (c/n 1072) is seen at the company base at Marana, Arizona, in October 1979. This aeroplane was later sold to the Argentine Navy.

Above: Seen landing at Miami in June 1989 is this **El Al Cargo** jumbo. Note only the word 'cargo' is displayed, a low profile is kept. 4X-AXF Boeing 747-258C (c/n 21594).

Below: Italian charter operator **Eurofly** has a fleet of four DC-9/MD-83 aircraft. I-FLYY Douglas DC-9-51 (c/n 47754) is about to depart Dublin, June 1994.

Below: **Estonian Aviation Company** – Elk Airways – operates this smartly painted Tupolev TU-154M ES-LTP (c/n 909). It is seen at the company base at Tallinn, May 1995. (J.D.S.)

Above: easyJet is a Luton, U.K.-based low-fare operator. It sells the seats direct to the public and advertises this fact by putting the booking telephone number in rather large letters on the cabin side. G-EZYA Boeing 737-3YO (c/n 23498) is at base, June 1996. (*P.E.P.*)

Above: Based at London–Gatwick **Euroair** used to fly commuter services. G-HGGS Embraer 110P1 Bandeirante (c/n 110294) visits Liverpool–Speke in April 1984. In 1988 the company ceased flying operations and now trades as an aircraft leasing company. (*J.D.S.*)

Below: **Forrestair Cargo** was an Australian operator flying services from Melbourne across the Bass Strait. VH-TAK Douglas DC-3 Dakota (c/n 13338) is at base, December 1979. The company had ceased operations in November of the previous year. (*R.O'B.*)

Below: **Eurocypria Airlines** is a Cyprus-based charter company. 5B-DBB Airbus A320-231 (c/n 256) arrives at Manchester–Ringway in March 1997. The company is a subsidiary of Cyprus Airways.

Below: **Eastern Airways** of Humberside, U.K., started operations in April 1972 as a charter carrier. It progressed to flying domestic scheduled passenger services. G-BKDO Short SD330 (c/n SH3091) is at Liverpool–Speke in October 1982. It was during this month that the airline merged with Genair.

Above: **East Line Aviation** of Moscow operates international charter and regional domestic scheduled services. RA76796 Ilyushin IL-76TD is on the cargo ramp at Sharjah, U.A.E., in March 1997.

Above: **East West Airlines** of Tamworth, N.S.W. Australia, flew Dakotas from 1953 to 1979. VH-AGU Douglas DC-3 (c/n 32668) was the last in service. It is at Melbourne–Essendon in December 1979. (*R.O'B.*)

Right: Frontier is a very popular name for an airline. First is a Denver, Colorado-based U.S. domestic carrier. N7354F Boeing 737-291 (c/n 22457) takes off from runway 16L at Seattle–Tacoma in September 1984. The company was merged into Continental in August 1986.

Above: British aerial survey company **Flight One** operates the Scottish Aviation Twin Pioneer CC2. G-AZHJ (c/n 577) is at Staverton, U.K., in July 1984.

Above: The second Frontier is **Frontier Flying Services** of Fairbanks, Alaska. It operates a mixed fleet with a DC-3 as the largest type. N59314 Douglas DC-3 Dakota (c/n 12363) is at Ryan Field, Arizona, in October 1979.

Below: Chilean cargo operator **Fast Air Carrier** flies re-engined 70 series DC-8s fitted with CFM56s. CC-CAR Douglas DC-8-71F (c/n 45976) approaches runway 9R at Miami, April 1994. The airline is a subsidiary of Lan Chile.

Above: **Flying Tigers** was founded in 1945 and was one of America's finest all-cargo airlines. N792FT Douglas DC-8-63CF (c/n 46046) lands at Miami, October 1981. The company merged into the Federal Express empire in August 1989.

Above: The third Frontier is a Canadian operator, **Frontier Air**, flying an assorted fleet from the company base in Ontario. C-GCTE Douglas DC-3 Dakota (c/n 13087) is at Oshkosh, Wisconsin, in August 1986. In January 1992 the carrier merged with Ontario Express to fly commuter services.

Below: The fourth **Frontier Airlines** is also a Denver-based U.S. domestic carrier. This operation started in 1994, subtitled 'The Spirit of the West'; each of the fleet has a very distinctive and different tail marking. N207AU Boeing 737-201 (c/n 19423) is at Phoenix–Sky Harbor, Arizona, in October 1996. (*J.D.S.*)

Below: Palma-based **Futura International Airways** is one of Spain's many holiday charter companies. EC-FYG Boeing 737-46B (c/n 24124) arrives at Manchester–Ringway in March 1995.

Above: Faucett Peru has a history going back to 1928. In a most striking colour scheme Lockheed L-1011 TriStar 50 OB-1545 (c/n 1075) lands on runway 9R at Miami in April 1994, with a backdrop of very dark rain-filled clouds.

Below: Fly Cruise is one of the 'brand' names of Carnival Airlines. The task is to fly holidaymakers to cruise ships. N6167D Boeing 727-282 (c/n 22430) lands at Miami, April 1994.

Below: Four Star Aviation of St Thomas in the U.S. Virgin Islands operates five freight Dakotas together with a few small passenger commuters. N132FS Douglas DC-3 Dakota (c/n 25778) is at San Juan, Puerto Rico, in November 1992.

Above: From the capital city, Helsinki, comes the national airline of Finland, **Finnair**. OH-LMY McDonnell Douglas MD-82 (c/n 53244) lands at London–Heathrow in October 1993.

Above: Miami has always been a home to a wide variety of small cargo carriers. Such a company is **Florida West Airlines**. N710FW Boeing 707-321C (c/n 20017) is at base, June 1989.

Below: It must take a character to name an operation **Flash Airlines**, but the company based in Bennin City, Nigeria, was such a carrier. 5N-ATZ Douglas DC-8F-55 (c/n 45965) departs London–Gatwick in July 1988. This company suspended services in October 1995.

Above: Fine Air of Miami operates a fleet of twelve DC-8 freighters. N426FB Douglas DC-8-54F (c/n 45667) is heading for the cargo area at base, November 1992.

Above: First Air is a division of Bradley Air Services of Canada flying both charter and scheduled operations. C-GVFA Boeing 727-44C (c/n 20475) is at Phoenix–Sky Harbor in September 1988.

67

Right: The Bolivian capital of La Paz is over 12,000 feet above sea level and does not have a wonderful road network. To service the need for fresh meat many operators fly an assortment of types to bring in freshly killed carcasses. One such carrier was **Fri Reyes** (Frigorifico Reyes). CP1434 Convair CV-240 (c/n 337) is at base, without engines, in November 1992. Two years later the airline ceased trading.

Above: Federal Express is a giant among small parcel carriers with a fleet running into hundreds. N68053 Douglas DC-10-10CF (c/n 47807) lands at Los Angeles–LAX in September 1988.

Below: Gulfstream International Airlines, despite the title, are a Miami-based commuter operator with a fleet of some twenty-five-plus aircraft. N198GA Beechcraft 1900C Airliner (c/n UB-5) is at base, April 1994.

Above: Seen here at Miami in August 1986, still in the colours of **Florida Airlines**, is Martin 404 N2589 (c/n 14232). The operator flew in the livery shown as well as 'Air South' and 'The Connection'. It was taken over by Air Florida.

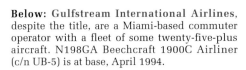

Above: Go Air used to specialise in V.I.P.-fitted Viscounts on lease to rock stars for their tours. N660RC Vickers Viscount 745D (c/n 229) is at the company H.Q. at Tucson in October 1984. During 1987 the company was sold to Jadepoint.

Below: Gull Air was a U.S. east-coast commuter line based at Hyannis, Massachusetts. N451AM Casa 212-200 (c/n 165) is seen at Boston in August 1986. In March the following year the company suspended operations.

Below: Based in the north-east of England at Newcastle, **Gill Airways** is a commuter line. G-OLAH Shorts SD360-100 (c/n SH3604) is on the ramp at Liverpool–Speke in June 1994.

Above: Based at Humberside in the east of England was commuter operator **Genair.** G-BHYT Embraer 110P1 Bandeirante (c/n 110277) is seen with its two PT6A turboprops running at Liverpool–Speke in June 1981. The airline suspended operations in July 1984.

Below: Great American Airways has had a steady yet slow growth since being founded in 1979, the year of deregulation. N1068T Douglas DC-9-15 (c/n 45782) is at home base of Reno Cannon, Nevada, in September 1988. Note how short the first series of DC-9 looks to the current MD models.

Below: With a mixed fleet of floatplane types **Green Airways** of Red Lake, Ontario, flies hunters and fishermen to remote cabins around the province. C-GEZU de Havilland (Canada) DHC2 Beaver (c/n 647) departs from Red Lake S.P.B. in June 1990.

Above: Germania are based at Berlin–Tegel with a growing fleet of 737s. Seen landing at Athens in June 1993 is D-AGEA Boeing 737-35B (c/n 23970).

Above: British independent operator **GB Airways** is one of a growing number of BA franchise airlines flying in BA colours. Seen landing at London–Heathrow in September 1993 is Boeing 737-236 G-BGDS (c/n 21806) in the company's own livery.

Above: Based in Bahrain, **Gulf Air** is a multinational airline covering the states of Oman, Abu Dhabi, Qatar and Bahrain. A40-EA Airbus A320-212 (c/n 313) lands at Athens in June 1993.

Above: Ghana Airways flies all its long-haul services with just two aircraft. 9G-ANA Douglas DC-10-30 (c/n 48286) is on the move at London–Heathrow in July 1993.

Left: Garuda Indonesia, flying from Jakarta, is the nation's largest airline operating worldwide with a fleet of over seventy-five of the latest Boeing and Airbus designs. PK-GSE Boeing 747-2U3B (c/n 22768) arrives at Zürich in August 1987.

69

Right: Auckland, New Zealand-based **Great Barrier Airlines** used to operate this rare antipodean design, the de Havilland DHA3 Drover, powered by three 145hp Gipsy Queen piston engines. A small number of the twenty Drovers built were re-engined with 180hp Lycomings. The aircraft illustrated, ZK-DDD (c/n 5019), is one such. Note the 'ZK' New Zealand register prefix is not carried; this is not unusual. (R.O'B.)

Above: Seen on a commuter flight to the world's busiest airport, Chicago–O'Hare, in March 1989 is **Great Lakes Aviation** Beechcraft 1900C Airliner N101BE (c/n UB-20). The company is based at Spencer, Iowa. In 1992 it became a United Express feeder and now flies in new livery. (S.G.W.)

Below: Cranways of Launceston, Tasmania, in 1980 formed **General Cargo Australia**. VH-SBL Douglas DC-3 Dakota (c/n 12056) is seen engineless in the company livery – it is hard to call it a colour scheme – at Melbourne–Essendon in June 1983 after trading had ceased. (R.O'B.)

Above: **German Cargo Services** was a subsidiary of Lufthansa but flew in its own livery. D-ABYW Boeing 747-230F (c/n 22669) lands at its Frankfurt base in September 1993. In the previous May the Company was renamed Lufthansa Cargo with the aircraft undergoing a repaint. (S.G.W.)

Above: **Gulf Air** again, but this Gulf is Mexico not Persian, and is an American independent based in Louisiana. N511GA Convair CV-580 (c/n 39) is visiting Philadelphia in January 1987. The airline was renamed Transocean Airways in 1989. (R.O'B.)

Below: From the British Channel Island of Guernsey comes this very smart Vickers Viscount 724 G-BDRC (c/n 52) of **Guernsey Airlines** on a scheduled service at Manchester–Ringway in July 1983. The carrier was merged into Air Europe Express in October 1989. (P.E.P.)

Below: The west has not gone in for building large-capacity civil helicopters so **Helitaxi Colombia** looked to Russia for its fleet of twenty-eight-seat Mil Mi-17s. HK3782X (c/n 95910) is at the company base of Bogota, November 1992.

Below: Seen at Washington–National in May 1989 is N902HA de Havilland (Canada) DHC7 Dash 7-102 (c/n 52) of **Henson Airlines** of Salisbury, Maryland. Note on the tail the marks of Allegheny Commuter. This operation evolved into USAir Express.

Above: HeavyLift Cargo Airlines of Stansted, U.K., specialise in the carriage of outsize loads that will not fit into a normal freight door. CCCP-76758 Ilyushin IL-76TD (c/n 0073474203) is at base, May 1992. The Russian aircraft is part of the operation run with Volga-Dnepr.

Below: Helicol of Colombia supplies both fixed- and rotary-wing aircraft to support the country's extensive oil industry. HK2970X de Havilland (Canada) DHC6 Twin Otter 300 (c/n 781) runs its two PT6A turboprops at Bogota in November 1992.

Above: A long way from jumbo jets are air taxi operators, but they still have a place in the market. HB-LOP Cessna 414 (c/n 414-0812) of **Horizon Air Taxi** is at the company base of Zürich in August 1987. In 1994 the airline dropped services and now only operates in a flight training role.

Below: Hapag–Lloyd is a major German charter company. The fleet can be seen at many of the world's holiday airports. D-AHLL Boeing 737-4K5 (c/n 24127) lands at Athens, June 1993.

Above: National airline of Vietnam was **Hang Khong Vietnam.** VN-A110 Tupolev TU-134A (c/n 62144) departs Bangkok in November 1989. Note the colour scheme is basic Aeroflot. The company now calls itself Vietnam Airlines.

Above: Spanish holiday charter operator **Hispania** flew this Sud Aviation SE210 Caravelle 10R EC-DCN (c/n 199). It is seen at Manchester–Ringway in September 1983. The airline suspended services in July 1989. *(J.D.S.)*

71

Below: Based in Honolulu **Hawaiian Air** flies a fleet of DC-9/DC-10 aircraft. N8969U Douglas DC-8-62 (c/n 46070) dates from August 1987 when it was in the fleet. It is seen a long way from home at Zürich.

Below: **Haiti Trans Air** operated passenger flights from Port-au-Prince to Miami in Peruvian-registered Boeing 727-247 OB-1301 (c/n 20263). The aircraft is seen at Miami in June 1989. Operations were suspended in October 1995.

Above: **Hamburg Airlines** is a commuter airline based in Germany. C-FCTD de Havilland (Canada) DHC8 Dash 8-102 (c/n 113) is at the Farnborough Air Show in September 1988, prior to lease by the carrier.

Above: Looking very smart at Kissimmee, Florida, in April 1994 is Sikorsky H34J N45726 (ex-56-4307) of **Hi-lift Helicopters International**. The locally based company had suspended services in 1992.

Above: **Highland Helicopters** of Vancouver, British Columbia, services the massive logging industry in the area. C-GLZG Bell 212 (c/n 31130) is lit by late-afternoon sun at base in September 1984.

Below: **Hinduja Cargo Services** was established in September 1996 with a majority share owned by Lufthansa. Its main operating bases are New Delhi and Sharjah, U.A.E. Boeing 727-243F N12411 (c/n 22052) is seen at the latter in March 1997.

Above: Seen at Miami in October 1981 is **Haiti Air Inter** de Havilland (Canada) DHC6 Twin Otter 200 HH-AIY (c/n 188). In 1984 the operator ceased trading and the aeroplane was sold to the air force.

Right: British operator **Hunting Cargo Airlines** is based at East Midlands–Castle Donington. It flies general cargo including overnight newspapers. G-FIJR Lockheed L-188PF Electra (c/n 1138) is at base, June 1996.

Above: As their name proclaims, **Holiday Airlines** of Istanbul flies charters to Turkey. Airbus A300B4-2C TC-RAE (c/n 029) arrives at Düsseldorf, July 1996. (*J.D.S.*)

Above: U.K. independent **Hot Air** was based at Southend. With its name it would have been the perfect operator to lease aircraft to politicians for election tours! G-BAPF Vickers Viscount 814 (c/n 338) is at Liverpool–Speke in May 1989. It was during this year that the airline merged into BAF. (*S.G.W.*)

Below: Seen on the ramp at Riga, Latvia, is YL-LBG Tupolev TU-134B-3 (c/n 63333). The aircraft is owned by Latavio but is marked as **Harco Air**, an airline from Kaduna, Nigeria. It had been on lease along with other TU-134s; these have all been returned and Harco Air now flies Boeing 727s. (*J.D.S.*)

Above: **The Hawaii Express** was a Los Angeles-based operation flying a daily low-fare service to Honolulu. Services started in August 1982 but ceased early in 1985. N905WA Douglas DC-10-10 (c/n 46938) is at Oakland, California, in January 1985. (*R.O'B.*)

Above: Harbor Airlines of Oak Harbor, Washington, operates a fleet of four commuter aircraft. N601DA Piper PA31-350 T1020 (c/n 31-8453002) is seen at Seattle–Tacoma in August 1992. (*R.O'B.*)

Below: Photographed at Auckland–Ardmore in March 1985 is ZK-EPF Bristol B170 Freighter Mk31M (c/n 13134) in the colours of **Hercules Airlines Ltd**. A fitting name for a type powered by Bristol Hercules 734 radial piston engines of 1,980hp. (*R.O'B.*)

Below: Canadian operator **Harbour Air** operates a fleet of twenty-five-plus single-engine floatplanes from its Vancouver base. C-FOCJ de Havilland (Canada) DHC2 Beaver (c/n 39) is at base, September 1992. (*R.O'B.*)

Right: IPEC (Interstate Parcel Express Company). The aviation division was formed in 1976 to fly from Melbourne to Tasmania with four flights a day. VH-IPF Douglas DC-9-33CF (c/n 47408) is at Melbourne–Essendon in June 1983. The carrier suspended operations in April 1993. (*R.O'B.*)

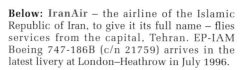

Above: Spanish national airline **Iberia** has been flying from Madrid since 1927. Boeing 757-256 EC-FXV (c/n 26241) arrives at London–Heathrow in June 1996 on one of the many daily flights from Spain.

Below: IranAir – the airline of the Islamic Republic of Iran, to give it its full name – flies services from the capital, Tehran. EP-IAM Boeing 747-186B (c/n 21759) arrives in the latest livery at London–Heathrow in July 1996.

Above: IcelandAir is the flag carrier for that nation and operates from its central location to both sides of the Atlantic. TF-FIJ Boeing 757-208 (c/n 25085) lands at London–Heathrow on a service from Reykjavik.

Above: : Acting as the freighter of the fleet, this Douglas DC-3 Dakota HK1149 (c/n 26593) of **Interandes Colombia** is at the carrier's base of Bogota in November 1992.

Below: Interconair – Irish Intercon Cattle Meats – operated a single Bristol 175 Britannia 235 EI-BBY (c/n 13455). The aircraft is seen at Luton, U.K., in April 1976. The aeroplane was destroyed in a landing accident at Shannon in September 1977. (*J.D.S.*)

Below: Iraqi Airways has not been allowed to fly, by United Nations order, since the Gulf War in 1991. YI-AGQ Boeing 727-270 (c/n 22261) shows off the company's smart livery at London–Heathrow in May 1988. (*S.G.W.*)

Above: **Intercontinental Colombia** flies a fleet of baby DC-9s. HK3710X Douglas DC-9-15 (c/n 45780) is at the gate awaiting passengers at Bogota in November 1992. It is of note that the seating capacity of a '15' series DC-9 is eighty-five people, the stretched MD-81 (DC-9-81) is 165.

Above: During the 1960s and the early 1970s most holiday charter flights were flown by old piston-engined types. Douglas DC-7B OY-ANA (c/n 45402) of **Internord** awaits the next passenger load at London–Gatwick in August 1968. The company flew both Danish- and Swedish-registered aircraft. Operations were suspended in December of that year. The aeroplane survived only a few more years before being broken up in France in 1973.

Below: Latvian freight operator **Inversija** has a fleet of four aircraft, three of which are IL-76s. YL-LAJ Ilyushin IL-76T (c/n 083414432) is at the company base of Riga in May 1995. (*J.D.S.*)

Below: Turkish operator **Istanbul Airlines**, based as named, flies a mixed all-Boeing fleet of 727/737/757. TC-APA Boeing 737-4S3 (c/n 25595) lands at London–Heathrow in October 1993.

Below: **Intereuropean Airways** was based at Cardiff in Wales, owned by a holiday company which flew its passengers to the sunspots of Europe. G-IEAC Boeing 757-236 (c/n 25620) lands at Manchester–Ringway in March 1993. In November of that year the company was taken over by Airtours.

Above: **Interflug** was the airline of the old G.D.R. – East Germany. DDR-SCX Tupolev TU-134A (c/n 48320) is on a rare visit to Manchester–Ringway in May 1988. After the Berlin Wall fell in November 1989 and Germany was reunited, the fate of the airline was sealed. In April 1991 flights were suspended and the company and the fleet of Russian-built aircraft were sold off.

Above: Local service Canadian operator **Intercity Airways** of Oshawa, Ontario, flew this Avro (HS) 748-244 Srs2 C-GLTC (c/n 1656). It is at base in July 1986. Operations ceased in October of that year.

Right: IAS (International Aviation Services) Cargo was a U.K. operator based at London–Gatwick. G-BEAF Boeing 707-321C (c/n 18591) is at Nairobi in March 1977. This aircraft is leased from Dan Air and carries both names. The airline was renamed British Cargo Airlines. (*R.O'B.*)

Above: Intercoastal Airways of Detroit–Willow Run is one of the few operators of the tall-tailed Douglas C-117D Super Dakota. N873SN (c/n 43327) is at base in July 1986. Three years later the fleet of two aircraft was sold.

Below: Intercontinental Airlines of Lagos, Nigeria, flew an assortment of cargo aircraft during the company's lifespan. 5N-AVR Douglas DC-8-52 (c/n 45758) is at Stansted, U.K., in May 1986. Operations were suspended late in 1990.

Above: State-owned Indian Airlines flies domestic and regional international passenger services. Airbus A300B4-203 VT-EHC (c/n 181) is on push-back at Sharjah, U.A.E., in March 1997.

Above: Seen on the ramp at Düsseldorf in July 1970 is Fokker F27-100 Friendship D-BAKI (c/n 10102) of German domestic passenger carrier IFG Inter Regional.

Below: Tehran-based Iran Asseman Airlines operates aircraft from nine to 184 seats. Aérospatiale ATR 72-212 EP-ATZ (c/n 398) is in the middle with seventy seats. It is seen landing at Dubai on a regular scheduled flight in March 1997.

Below: German commuter airline Interot flies services from Augsburg. D-BIER de Havilland (Canada) DHC8 Dash 8-103 (c/n 310) is on a service at Düsseldorf in May 1995. On 1 January 1996 the carrier was renamed Augsburg Airways. (*P.E.P.*)

Above: Ilavia is a sister company of the Ilyushin OKB (Experimental Design Bureau). Needless to say it operates Ilyushin-built aircraft from the company base at the Zhukovsky test airfield. IL-76TD RA76473 (c/n 0033448404) is seen operating a cargo flight at Sharjah, U.A.E., in March 1997.

Above: Operating from Dublin **Iona National Airways** provided air taxi and charter flights. EI-BGP Cessna 414A (c/n 414A-0016) visits Liverpool–Speke for a horse race in April 1986. Operations closed down in December 1994.

Below: Jersey Airlines was founded in 1948 in the Channel Islands. Over the following years it grew, operating scheduled flights around the U.K. and France. In 1962, following the sale to the holding company of BUA, the airline became British United (C.I.) Airways. Seen here at the Biggin Hill Air Show in June 1996 is G-AORG de Havilland DH114 Heron 2B (c/n 14101) in full Jersey Airlines colours, as the aircraft used to look when operated by the company between 1956 to 1961. It is now privately owned by a preservation group and attends air shows. (*S.G.W.*)

Below: British carrier **InterCity Airlines** of East Midlands–Castle Donington was a commuter line. It flew contract services for the Scottish oil industry as well as scheduled services from E.M.A. G-BITV Shorts SD330-200 (c/n SH3068) is at Manchester–Ringway in May 1981. Operations ceased in August 1983. (*P.E.P.*)

Below: Inex – Adria was a Yugoslavian charter operator based in Ljubljana. YU-AHW Douglas DC-9-33 (c/n 47530) is at Manchester–Ringway in October 1982. The break-up of that country has found the airline in the new country of Slovenia with a new registration letter 'S5', a new livery, and the name changed to Adria.

Above: Imair is an airline based in Baku, Azerbaijan, an ex-Soviet republic. 4K-85524 Tupolev TU-154B-2 (c/n 524) is at Sharjah in March 1997. The carrier's colours are still basic Aeroflot with a registration prefix change and the republic's flag on the cabin roof.

Above: Based in Bucharest, Romanian airline **Jaro International** has a mixed fleet of BAC 111/B-707 passenger and cargo aircraft. YR-JBB BAC 111-528FL (c/n 238) arrives at Düsseldorf in July 1996. (*J.D.S.*)

Right: JetAire Airlines of Albuquerque, New Mexico, flew two of the original Handley Page-built Jetstreams. The airline suspended flights in January 1986. N114CP Handley Page HP137 Jetstream Mk1 (c/n 202) is at base in October 1984. This mark of Jetstream was fitted with two Astazou turboprops; later BAe-built aircraft had Garrett TPE331 engines. (The formation flying in the background is the U.S.A.F. team The Thunderbirds.)

Above: Japan Air Systems is largely a domestic operator. JA8062 McDonnell Douglas MD-90-30 (c/n 53352) is the new type in the new colours. It is seen at Osaka–Itami in October 1996. (*R.O'B.*)

Above: Seen landing at Hong Kong in February 1996 is **Japan Asia Airways** Douglas DC-10-40 JA8532 (c/n 46660). The company is a subsidiary of JAL, and was formed to operate services to Taiwan so as not to upset the Beijing government. (*J.D.S.*)

Below: Japan Air Cargo Boeing 747-246F JA8151 (c/n 22477) on the runway at London–Heathrow in July 1993. Note the company name is JA Cargo not JAL Cargo, and the removal of the tail logo and replacement with an oversize registration.

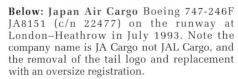

Above: Jersey European Airways is based at Exeter in the west of England, not on the island of Jersey. It flies scheduled services around the U.K. G-OLCA BAe 146-200 (c/n E2099) is at London–Gatwick in August 1993. Note the tail logo is like a B-2 bomber silhouette.

Above: Japan Air Lines is the country's long-haul operator. JA8074 Boeing 747-446 (c/n 24426) arrives at London–Heathrow in July 1995.

Below: Japan Air Commuter is a subsidiary of JAS NAMC YS11A-500 JA8763 (c/n 2135), in what used to be a shared basic colour scheme with JAS, is at Osaka–Itami in October 1996. (*R.O'B.*)

Below: Swiss airline **JU-Air** flies the three Junkers Ju52/3m aircraft obtained from the Swiss Air Force, which had got them new in 1939. The airline provides pleasure flights through, not over, the Alps. HB-HOP (c/n 6610) lands at Zürich in August 1987.

Below: JAT (Jugoslavenski Aero Transport) was formed in 1947 as the national airline. Today the country is only part of what it used to be but JAT is still serving what is left. YU-ANK Boeing 737-3H9 (c/n 23715) lands at London–Heathrow in July 1995.

Above: British operator **Kestrel Airways** was formed in 1970 with a single DC-3. Most flying took the form of ad hoc freight and passenger charters. G-AMFV Douglas DC-3 Dakota (c/n 10105) is at East Midlands–Castle Donington in April 1971. The Dakota was sold in August 1972 and all flying was suspended in November of that year.

Below: **Kitty Hawk Air Cargo** of Dallas, Texas, flies a mix of jet and jetprop freight aircraft. N94235 Convair CV-600 (c/n 68) is at Tucson is September 1988. The engines have been removed on this aircraft. The CV-600 is a re-engine conversion with a pair of Rolls-Royce Dart turboprops.

Above: **Kibris Turkish Airlines** is part owned by THY and the government of North Cyprus, a state recognised only by Turkey. TC-JYK Airbus A310-203 (c/n 172) arrives at London–Heathrow in June 1996.

Below: This Kiwi is a New Zealand one, but in a hybrid colour scheme. **Kiwi Travel International Airlines** of Hamilton leased this Air 2000 aircraft for the southern hemisphere summer. G-OOOU Boeing 757-2Y0 (c/n 25240) is at Manchester–Ringway in May 1996 at the end of the lease. It has Kiwi titles and tail logo. The airline had operated low-cost services and ceased trading in September 1996.

Above: Seen arriving at London–Heathrow in June 1996 is this Airbus A340-313 9K-ANB (c/n 090) of **Kuwait Airways** on a direct flight from Kuwait City.

Above: **Kiwi International Airlines** is in fact a U.S. scheduled passenger carrier based in Newark, New Jersey. N360PA Boeing 727-230 (c/n 20676) is at Tampa, Florida, in April 1994.

Right: Kyrgyzstan Airlines is the airline of the ex-U.S.S.R. republic of the same name. Based in Bishkek, services are flown to Moscow–Domodedovo. EX85252 Tupolev TU-154B-1 (c/n 252) arrives at Moscow in August 1995 in a colour scheme that is still recognisable as ex-Aeroflot.

Above: New Russian airline Krai Aero is based at Moscow–Vnukovo. RA85803 Tupolev TU-154M (c/n 822) is at base in August 1995.

Above: Based in Salt Lake City, Utah, Key Airlines flew general contract and charter flights. One particular service was for the U.S. Navy to ferry between Point Magu N.A.S. and San Nicolas Island, two bases in California. N30KA Convair CV-440 (c/n 364) is at Oxnard, California, in October 1979.

Below: Korean Airlines is one of the largest international carriers in Asia. HL7456 Boeing 747SP-B5 (c/n 22483) lands at New York–J.F.K. in May 1989. The short-body S.P. (Special Performance) jumbo was designed for very long non-stop flights.

Above: In 1987 World Airways took over control of Key. The base was moved to Las Vegas and the fleet became all-B-727. N29KA Boeing 727-51 (c/n 18803) is at New York–J.F.K. in May 1989. It shows off the new livery and the new name of Key Air.

Above: This Korean Air Lines Cargo Boeing 707-373C shows off the previous colours the carrier wore. N370WA (c/n 19442) is at Bahrain in May 1977. (*R.O'B.*)

Below: With a history going back to 1920 KLM (Koninklijke Luchtvaart Maatschappij) can claim over seventy-five years of constant service. (The carrier had a service running in the Dutch West Indies during World War Two, so even though the European service stopped, KLM flew on.) PH-DTB Douglas DC-10-30 (c/n 46551) arrives at Caracas in November 1992.

Below: Kalitta of Detroit–Willow Run is well located to fly motor industry parts around the country. The large aircraft fly as American International Airways and the small as Kalitta Flying Service. N231SK Volpar Turboliner (c/n AF856) is at base in June 1990. The Volpar is a radical conversion of a Beech 18, giving it turboprops, tricycle undercarriage and a deeper fuselage.

Above: Kenya Airways was formed in 1977 and is government-owned. Scheduled passenger services are flown to other African and European countries. 5Y-BEL Airbus A310-304 (c/n 416) is on the move at London–Heathrow in August 1989.

Below: Kabo Air is a Nigerian domestic passenger airline based in the town of Kano. 5N-AWX Boeing 727-25 (c/n 18256) is at Opa Locka, Florida, in May 1989 after being withdrawn from use.

Below: Finnish airline **Kar Air** was formed in 1957 and flew scheduled domestic and international charters. OH-KDC Douglas DC-6B (c/n 44169) is at London–Gatwick in August 1969. The airline was owned by Finnair which eventually absorbed them in May 1996. (*S.G.W.*)

Above: KAL Aviation is an Athens-based air taxi operator. SX-DKA Britten-Norman BN2B-27 Islander (c/n 2114) lands at base in June 1993.

Below: Kazakhstan is yet another ex-Soviet republic. From the capital Almaty comes this **Kazakstan Airlines** Ilyushin IL-86 UN86068 (c/n 51483204035) seen on a passenger flight to Sharjah in March 1997. The carrier had been declared bankrupt by the government late in 1996. The assets were to be transferred to a newly named operator, Air Kazakhstan. As this photograph was taken several months after this should have taken place, what is happening is unclear.

Above: Kelner Airways Limited was based at Pickle Lake in northern Ontario. It flew all types of cargo and passengers around that remote region. C-GLTC Avro (HS) 748-244 Srs 2 (c/n 1656) is being loaded at base in June 1990. A new name, Wasaya Airways, was adopted in January 1993.

Above: Russian operator **Kras Air** (Krasnoyarsk Airlines) is based in the city of that name. It has a mixed passenger/cargo fleet of over fifty aircraft. RA76465 Ilyushin IL-76TD (c/n 0023438101) is still in basic Aeroflot marks at Sharjah in March 1997.

Below: Libyan Arab Airlines took the present name after the 1969 revolution. 5A-DIG Boeing 727-2L5 (c/n 21333) is at London–Heathrow in June 1978. Since April 1992 no Libyan flights have been allowed out of the country because of U.N. sanctions.

Below: LOT (Polskie Linie Lotnicze) was formed in 1929; owned by the Polish government it flies worldwide. SP-LCA Tupolev TU-154M (c/n 727) is at London–Heathrow in May 1988. With the political changes in recent years the company fleet is getting more westernised.

Above: Libyan Arab Air Cargo is the all-freight division of LAA. Tripoli-based, it too can only fly domestic operations. 5A-DNA Ilyushin IL-76TD (c/n 0023439140) is at Moscow–Bykovo in August 1995. It has been stored there for some years.

Above: Portuguese domestic operator LAR (Ligacões Aereas Regionais) was set up in 1985 to link the capital city, Lisbon, with major provincial cities. CS-TAG Avro (HS) 748 Srs2A-270 (c/n 1687) is at East Midlands–Castle Donington in July 1990. The airline was renamed Euroair in March 1993.

Below: A very tranquil setting for Lac Seul Airways de Havilland (Canada) DHC3 Otter C-FPEN (c/n 439) as it sits at Lac Seul S.P.B., Ear Falls, Ontario, in June 1990. The operator flies fishermen and hunters to remote log cabins.

Above: Vilnius-based Lithuanian Airlines is flag carrier for the newly independent Baltic state. LY-AAX Yakovlev YAK-42D (c/n 4520424811431) shows off the bright company colours at London–Heathrow, June 1994. (J.D.S.)

Above: Frankfurt-based Lufthansa Cargo operates a hub at Sharjah with at least two flights a day. D-ABZB Boeing 747-230F (c/n 23348) arrives at Sharjah in March 1997 with a cargo load.

Above: LAC – Lineas Aereas Canedo – is a Bolivian passenger charter company flying executive configured aircraft. CP2237 Convair CV-340 (c/n 228) sits on the company ramp at Cochabamba in immaculate condition in November 1992.

Above: Based at La Paz, Bolivia, **LAI** – Linea Aerea Imperial – operated from El Alto airport at a height of 13,500 feet above sea level. CP1635 Swearingen SA226TC Metro II (c/n TC-359) is on the military ramp at base in November 1992 following suspension of services during the previous year.

Above: In the brief time since independence, the Baltic state of Latvia has acquired a number of airlines. Largest of them is Riga-based **Latavio**. YL-LBI Tupolev TU-134B-3 (c/n 63365) is on a service to London–Gatwick in August 1993.

Below: LTE International Airways is a Spanish charter company with a fleet of three 757s. The airline is an associate of the German LTU company, the basic colour scheme being the same. EC-EFX Boeing 757-2G5 (c/n 23118) arrives at Manchester–Ringway, July 1993.

Below: With a fleet of two Dakotas **Lacol – Colombia** (Lineas Aereas Colombianas) is based at Villavicencio where it flies assorted cargo services. HK124 Douglas DC-3 Dakota (c/n 4349) is seen visiting Bogota in November 1992.

Above: LTU Sud International Airlines is a south German-based charter company. The airline is part of the LTU group. D-AMUU Boeing 757-225 (c/n 22688) lands at Athens, June 1993.

Below: Leisure Air was an American operator with an all-Airbus fleet. Based in Winston-Salem, North Carolina, the airline suspended services in February 1995. N317RX Airbus A320-231 (c/n 317) arrives at Tampa in April 1994.

Left: Lionair was a passenger charter airline owned by Luxair and Cargolux. LX-GCV Boeing 747-121 (c/n 19660) is at Manchester–Ringway in June 1988 while on charter to Orionair. Late in 1990 the aircraft were sold off.

Right: Flying from the heart of Europe is **Luxair**, airline of the Grand Duchy of Luxembourg. Now flying 737s and Fokker 50s, it used to operate the greatest of all the propliners, the Lockheed L-1649A Starliner. LX-LGY (c/n 1036) is on a service to London–Gatwick in August 1968.

Above: Yet another Leisure, this one is a U.K. holiday airline flying to Europe and the U.S.A. **Leisure International Airways** operates out of London–Gatwick and Manchester–Ringway. G-UKLI Boeing 767-39H (c/n 26257) is seen landing at the latter airport in August 1995. The company is a subsidiary of Air UK.

Below: The Caravelle is quickly disappearing from the sky. Those flying are more and more likely to be in remote places. **Lineas Aereas Suramericanas – Colombia** is a freight operator based in Bogota. HK3756X Sud Aviation SE210 Caravelle 10B3 (c/n 259) is at base in November 1992.

Above: Being worked on at its Bogota base is this tall-tailed Super Dakota. It is the sole fleet of **LADU Colombia** (Linea Aerea de Uraba). HK3586 Douglas C-117D (c/n 43325) is photographed in November 1992. The airline ceased operations in 1995.

Above: London City Airways was an airline for business people to fly into the capital's financial district (London City airport). The attractive tail logo must make the busy executive feel at home. G-BOAX de Havilland (Canada) DHC7 Dash 7-110 (c/n 111) is at East Midlands–Castle Donington in July 1989. The airline was part of the Airlines of Great Britain Group and was merged into the main unit, British Midland, in October 1990.

Below: Based at Barranquilla on Colombia's Caribbean Sea coast is **LAC** – Lineas Aereas del Caribe – a cargo airline. HK2632X Douglas DC-8F-53 (c/n 45768) is at Miami, October 1981.

Below: Lacsa – Lineas Aereas de Costa Rica – flies passengers from San José to a number of locations around North and South America. N1280E Boeing 727-2Q6 (c/n 21972) is at Miami, October 1981.

Above: Seen in temporary store at Opa Locka, Florida, in October 1981 is this Curtiss C-46D Commando CC-CDC (c/n 30653) of **Linea Aerea Sud-Americana**, a Chilean freight company based in Santiago.

Below: Lacsa Carga flew this Douglas DC-8-55F N29549 (c/n 45803) on dedicated cargo services. It is seen at Miami in June 1989.

Above: Lincoln Airlines was a freight operator based at Indianapolis. N584PL Convair CV-580 (c/n 115) is seen at Opa Locka in April 1994. The airline had suspended services in 1990.

Right: Ladeco Cargo is the freight arm of the main carrier. Note a totally different livery. CC-CYA Boeing 707-327C (c/n 19530) lands on runway 9R at Miami in April 1994. In October of that year the cargo unit suspended operations.

Below: From its formation in 1955, Düsseldorf-based **LTU** (Luft Transport Unternehmen) has grown to be a giant in German holiday charter flying. D-ABAX Fokker F28 Fellowship 1000 (c/n 11006) is at Frankfurt, July 1970.

Below: Chilean airline **Ladeco** (Linea Aerea del Cobre) flies passengers from Santiago around South America and Florida. CC-CHC Boeing 727-95 (c/n 19251) is at Miami in June 1989.

Above: LanChile was formed by the government in 1929 and took the present name in 1932. The airline flies passengers worldwide. CC-CEU Boeing 767-33A (c/n 25403) lands at Miami in April 1994.

Right: Vienna-based **Lauda Air** was formed in 1979 by Formula One racing driver Niki Lauda to fly charters. The airline has grown large enough to be able to order B-777s. Besides the holiday charters, scheduled services have been added in association with Lufthansa. OE-ILG Boeing 737-3Z9 (c/n 24081) is at London–Gatwick in August 1993.

Above: Freight services are operated by **Lan Chile Cargo**. CC-CEB Boeing 707-385C (c/n 19000) is at Miami in June 1989. In January 1991 the aircraft was sold to the Chilean Air Force and the company no longer has a dedicated cargo aircraft.

Below: Bolivian meat freighter **La Cumbre** (Transportes Aereos La Cumbre) had a fleet of two DC-6s. CP1282 Douglas DC-6A (c/n 45530) is at company base, La Paz, in November 1992. As can be seen corporate image was not a priority. Operations were suspended in 1995.

Above: French airline **L'Aeropostale** is based at Paris–C.D.G. with a fleet of 727/737 aircraft. Seen arriving at Athens in June 1993 is F-GFUF Boeing 737-3B3 (c/n 24388).

Above: **Laker Airways** was founded by one of the great characters of British commercial aviation, Mr Freddie Laker, in 1966. The company flew holiday charters to the sunspots of Europe. G-AVBX BAC 111-320AZ (c/n 109) is at the company base, London–Gatwick, in August 1968. It was a sad day for many when in February 1982 services were suspended.

Below: **Loganair**, Scotland's airline, is based in Glasgow and flies schedule services around the U.K. G-OLCD BAe ATP (c/n 2018) is on the runway at Manchester–Ringway in April 1991. The company has entered into a franchise agreement with BA and now flies in the livery of BA Express.

Below: Just to prove you cannot keep a good man down, Laker is back. In 1992 **Laker Airways (Bahamas)** was formed to fly from Freeport to Fort Lauderdale, and in 1995 came Laker Airways which was based at the latter. N833LA Douglas DC-10-30 (c/n 46958) arrives at Manchester–Ringway in June 1996 from Florida on a holiday charter.

Above: Lufthansa CityLine is the commuter arm of the airline. Note the different tail logo. D-AFKC Fokker 50 (c/n 20121) arrives at Manchester–Ringway in May 1992.

Above: LAB – Lloyd Aereo Boliviano – is another South American airline with a long history that dates back to 1925. The carrier is government owned. CP2232 Airbus A310-304 (c/n 562) is on the ramp at the company base of Cochabamba in November 1992. Note that in the absence of air bridge boarding, to ensure people do not go to the wrong aircraft on the ramp, a sign is at the foot of the steps to denote destination.

Below: LIAT – The Caribbean Airline is the new name for Leeward Islands Air Transport Service. The company is owned by the various island governments and flies from Antigua to over twenty other islands with scheduled services. V2-LCY de Havilland (Canada) DHC8 Dash 8-110 (c/n 035) arrives at St Thomas, B.V.I., in April 1989. (*S.G.W.*)

Below: One of the best known airlines of the world is German operator **Lufthansa**, which flies a large fleet across the world. D-ADFO Douglas DC-10-30 (c/n 47925) is at Toronto in July 1986.

Below: **Lloyd Aereo Boliviano Cargo** operates a single aircraft, a dedicated freight carrier. CP1365 Boeing 707-323C (c/n 18692) lands at Miami, June 1989.

Above: With a fleet of four aircraft **Lat Charter** flies from the Latvian capital, Riga. YL-LBE Tupolev TU-134B-3 (c/n 63285) is seen climbing out from Sharjah, U.A.E., in March 1997.

Above: **Lanica** (Lineas Aereas de Nicaragua) used to be the airline of that country. AN-BFN Douglas DC-6B (c/n 45322) gets a car loaded into the freight door at Miami in August 1976. The operator started services in 1945 with the assistance of Pan Am and was declared insolvent in March 1981. For many years the carrier was owned, through a holding company, by the Somoza family who ruled the country until the 1979 revolution. It is of note that the country registration letter has since changed from 'AN' to 'YN'. (*R.O'B.*)

Right: Argentine commuter line **LAER** (Lineas Aereas Entre Rios) is based at Parana. LV-VEI BAe 3212 Jetstream Super 31 (c/n 830) shows off its very smart livery at Buenos Aires Aeroparque in November 1994. (*R.O'B.*)

Above: British independent airline **Lakeside Northwest** flew this BAe 3012 Jetstream 31 G-LAKJ (c/n 626). It is seen at Liverpool–Speke awaiting the next passenger load in October 1993; the following month operations were suspended. (*J.D.S.*)

Above: **LAPA** (Lineas Aereas Privadas Argentinas) flies services from Buenos Aires Aeroparque. LV-VGF Boeing 737-2M6 (c/n 21138) is on the runway at base in June 1994. (*R.O'B.*)

Below: Miami-based **Millon Air** operates a fleet of six aircraft for general ad hoc cargo work. N722GS Boeing 707-321C (c/n 19373) is loaded at base in June 1989.

Above: **Lao Aviation** Boeing 737-291 RDPL-34125 (c/n 20363) is at Bangkok in February 1996. The carrier is the national flag carrier of Laos and is based in the capital, Vientiane. (*R.O'B.*)

Above: **MEA** – Middle East Airlines – is one of the last, if not *the* last, passenger operators of the Boeing 707. Plenty of 707s still fly cargo, but not passengers. The Beirut carrier can now only fly them into airports without strict noise regulations. OD-AGV Boeing 707-347C (c/n 19967) lands at London–Heathrow in September 1993. Airbus A310s are now used on the route.

Below: The country of Myanmar used to be known as Burma. With the current dictatorship it is not very easy to visit. The national airline **Myanma Airways** flies to surrounding countries. XY-AGA Fokker F28 Fellowship 4000 (c/n 11232) departs Bangkok in November 1989.

Below: Wisconsin-based **Midstate Airlines** flew commuter passengers around the state and beyond. N192MA Swearingen SA227AC Metro III (c/n AC-476) departs Oshkosh in August 1986. The carrier suspended services in January 1989.

Above: Flying small overnight parcels, **Mid-Atlantic Freight** of Greensboro, North Carolina, has a fleet of over twenty aircraft. Cessna 208 Caravan 1 N9639F (c/n 208-00121) is at Dothan–Napier, Alabama, in April 1994. The entire fleet is made up of this new workhorse turboprop.

Below: Monarch Airlines of Luton, U.K., is a major player in both long- and short-haul holiday charters. G-DAJB Boeing 757-2T7 (c/n 23770) lands at Manchester–Ringway in April 1993.

Above: Mey-Air was an Oslo, Norway-based charter operator. LN-MTC Boeing 737-201 (c/n 20453) departs Palma, Majorca, in November 1973. Boeing repossessed the aircraft in March 1974, the carrier having ceased operations the previous month.

Below: Turkish airline **Mas Air** is based at Istanbul and mainly flies helicopters. Fixed-wing operations were flown by two aircraft leased from Aeroflot. TC-MOB Antonov AN-24RV (c/n 27307608) is seen back at the end of the lease at Moscow–Bykovo in August 1995.

Below: Engineless and in store at Tamiami, Florida, in April 1994 is **Maya Caga International** Douglas DC-6A XA-RIK (c/n 44600). The aircraft was once owned by Rich and still has signs of its colour scheme. The carrier, which had just one aircraft, suspended operations in 1991.

Above: Iranian carrier **Mahan Air** flies passengers and cargo from its base in the city of Kerman. Tupolev TU-154M EP-JAZ (c/n 898) arrives at Dubai, U.A.E., in March 1997.

Above: Seen on the ramp at Johannesburg–Jan Smuts in May 1986 is ZS-LGP Embraer 110P1 Bandeirante (c/n 110402) of **Mmabaho Air Services** of Mafeking. The following year the name Bopair (Mafeking is in the Republic of Bophuthatswana, at one time a semi-independent tribal homeland) was introduced. (*R.O'B.*)

Right: American non-scheduled airline **Modern Air Transport** operated I/T flights from Berlin in the early 1970s. Seen at Palma, Majorca, in November 1973 is N5623 Convair CV-990-30A (c/n 20). The CV-990 and its predecessor the CV-880 racked up massive losses for the manufacturer as they failed to sell in any great numbers, being overshadowed by the B-707 and the DC-8; it was, however, the fastest of them all. Modern Air suspended operations late in 1975.

Above: Danish airline **Maersk Air** flies a mix of schedules and charters from its Copenhagen base. A British subsidiary operates as a BA franchise company at Birmingham. OY-APW Boeing 720-051B (c/n 18422) is at Palma, Majorca, in November 1973 showing off the all blue colours of the company.

Below: **Muse Air** was started in 1981 by the family who had made Southwest the company it is today. N931MC McDonnell Douglas MD-82 (c/n 48057) is at Los Angeles (LAX) in October 1984. Southwest purchased the company in March of 1985 and renamed it Transtar.

Above: **MMA** – McRobertson Miller Airlines – of Perth, Western Australia, flew scheduled passenger services. VH-FKC Fokker F28 Fellowship (c/n 11025) is under final assembly at Schiphol, July 1970. The company had been part of the Ansett Group since 1963, and in 1981 became Ansett W.A.

Above: The Republic of Macedonia is another ex-Yugoslavian country. **Meta AvioTransport Macedonia** was formed in 1992 with two leased TU-154 aircraft. Operations were suspended in January 1994. RA85619 Tupolev TU-154M (c/n 738) is parked at Moscow–Vnukovo in August 1995. The aircraft was leased from Vnukovo Airways, and it is a pity that such a wonderful colour scheme is no longer flying.

Below: **Malaysian Airlines** is one of Asia's largest carriers. From the main base at Kuala Lumpur it flies extensive Asian operations together with worldwide services. 9M-MPG Boeing 747-4H6 (c/n 25703) lands at London–Heathrow in July 1995.

Below: **MK Airlines** is a freight operator based at London–Gatwick but flying DC-8s registered in Ghana and Nigeria. 9G-MKE Douglas DC-8F-55 (c/n 45753) is seen on the cargo ramp at Sharjah, U.A.E., in March 1997.

Above: Coventry, U.K.-based **MAC** (Midland Air Charter) had two claims to fame: the first was that it was aristocratic, having been formed by a lord and a marquis; the second that it was the world's last operator of the long-nose Bristol B170 Super Freighter Mk32. G-APAV (c/n 13263) is at base in May 1973. The previous February operations had been suspended. (*S.G.W.*)

Below: Formed in 1958 as Martin's Air Charter, today's name of **Martinair** came into being in 1974. The airline is a leading Dutch charter operator; KLM are a shareholder. PH-MBT Douglas DC-10-30F (c/n 46985) lands at New York–J.F.K. in May 1989.

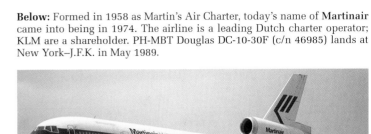

Below: Morton Air Services was formed by Captain Morton at the end of World War Two making it one of Britain's oldest independents. Scheduled services were flown to France and the Channel Islands. G-AMRA Douglas DC-3 Dakota (c/n 26735) is at London–Gatwick in July 1968. In November of that year the company joined British United. (*S.G.W.*)

Above: From the Republic of China (Taiwan) comes **Mandarin Airlines,** a subsidiary of China Airlines. B152 McDonnell Douglas MD-11 (c/n 48470) is at Schiphol, August 1995. (*P.E.P.*)

Above: McCulloch International Airlines was an operator of the Lockheed L-188A Electra from 1971 to 1978. N6310A (c/n 1121) is at Chicago–Midway in August 1970. The carrier filed for bankruptcy upon the death of the principal owner in 1977. (*S.G.W.*)

Above: Mackey International Airlines was based at Fort Lauderdale, Florida. N441JM Convair CV-440 (c/n 435) is at base in July 1974. Operations were suspended in 1980. (*S.G.W.*)

Below: Metropolitan Airways of Bournemouth, U.K., was an early example of a franchise operator. G-BELS de Havilland (Canada) DHC6 Twin Otter 300 (c/n 530) is at Manchester–Ringway, June 1982, in the livery of a Dan Air City Link. Metropolitan ceased operations at the end of August 1985. (*P.E.P.*)

Left: One of the last operators of the Martin 404 was **Marco Island Airways** of Marco Island, Florida. N968M (c/n 14159) is at Opa Locka in July 1974. The company was taken over by PBA in 1985. (*S.G.W.*)

Right: **MGM Grand Air** operated a New York–J.F.K. to Los Angeles–LAX service with a difference. The 727 might be normal on the outside, but inside in place of 130-plus normal seats is a thirty-three-seat luxury cabin divided into four staterooms. N503MG Boeing 727-191 (c/n 19392) is visiting Manchester–Ringway on charter to a popular music group in July 1992. The airline was bought for the fleet by Kalitta – American International in December 1994. (*J.D.S.*)

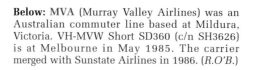

Above: Operating just one aircraft, **Merchant Express Aviation** of Lagos, Nigeria, flies cargo from Africa to Europe and back. 5N-MXX Boeing 707-323C (c/n 18940) is at Ostend, Belgium, in July 1996. (*P.E.P.*)

Below: **MVA** (Murray Valley Airlines) was an Australian commuter line based at Mildura, Victoria. VH-MVW Short SD360 (c/n SH3626) is at Melbourne in May 1985. The carrier merged with Sunstate Airlines in 1986. (*R.O'B.*)

Above: Farmington, New Mexico, is the home of **Mesa Airlines**, a large western commuter line. N5YV Beechcraft 1900D Airliner (c/n UE-5) is at Phoenix–Sky Harbor in October 1992. (*J.D.S.*)

Above: Alaskan-based **Markair** started by running both schedule and ad hoc cargo services; passengers were added later. N108AK Lockheed L-100-30 Hercules (c/n 4610) is at Detroit–Willow Run in August 1986. Services were suspended in October 1995. (*J.D.S.*)

Below: The commuter arm of Markair was based at a different location, Berthel as opposed to Anchorage. **Markair Express** de Havilland (Canada) DHC6 Twin Otter 300 N723CA (c/n 723) is seen at Anchorage, July 1992. Like the main company it also suspended operations in October 1995. (*R.O'B.*)

Below: Russian start-up operator is **Moscow Airways**, based at the city's Sheremetyevo airport. RA11318 Antonov AN-12 (c/n 401908) is at base in August 1995. From a mixed fleet of seven aircraft six are cargo carriers. (*J.D.S.*)

Above: Millardair of Toronto was once a leading charter and cargo operator with an all-propliner fleet. C-GQIB Douglas C-54E Skymaster (c/n 27370) is at base in June 1990. This was the month services were suspended due to not being able to get take-off slots, as required, to handle urgent cargo loads. The cargo fleet was stored and then sold off.

Below: Based in Skopje is **Macedonian Airlines**. Once part of Yugoslavia, the new republic leases aircraft to operate the services. Yakovlev YAK-42 RA42326 (c/n 4520424402154) arrives at Düsseldorf in July 1996. (*J.D.S.*)

Below: Mexicana (Compania Mexicana de Aviación) have a history going back to 1921, and thus can claim to be one of the world's oldest airlines. N553NA Boeing 727-2J7 (c/n 20707) arrives at Los Angeles–LAX in September 1988. The company flies passengers to the U.S.A. and Central America as well as domestic operations.

Above: Midway was one of the airlines that grew using the older inner city airports rather than the big new ones many miles out; in this case it was Chicago's Midway airport. N937ML Douglas DC-9-31 (c/n 47005) is at Washington National in May 1989. In March 1991 the company filed for relief under Chapter 11 of bankruptcy law and continued until November of that year when operations ceased. In 1993 a completely new company, same name and address, started services.

Below: Miami Air started operations with a fleet of 727s in 1991. N804MA Boeing 727-225 (c/n 22435) arrives back at base in late evening sun in November 1992.

Above: Italian passenger airline **Meridiana** has a fleet mix of BAe146/DC-9s. McDonnell Douglas MD-82 HB-IKL (now I-SMEM) (c/n 49248) arrives at Athens in June 1993.

Above: Mid-Pacific Air started in 1980 as a low-fare, high-frequency passenger service from Honolulu to the other islands. At the end of the decade the company moved to Lafayette, Indiana, as a cargo carrier. N125MP NAMC YS-11A-310 (c/n 2070) is at Detroit–Willow Run in June 1990. Operations were suspended in 1995.

Right: U.K. operator **Manx Airlines** is based on the Isle of Man, an offshore banking centre and holiday resort. G-BFZL Vickers Viscount 836 (c/n 436) departs Liverpool–Speke on a scheduled service to the island, August 1988. The airline is part of the same group as British Midland; some services are run as a BA Express franchise.

Above: Founded in 1946 Hungarian national airline **Malev** (Magyar Legikozlekedisi Vallalat) flies around Europe and the Middle East. Like most operators from eastern Europe the fleet mix is now swinging towards western-built aircraft. HA-LCG Tupolev TU-154B (c/n 127) is at Zürich, August 1987.

Below: New Zealand carrier **Mount Cook Airlines** operates from a number of centres in the country and flies aircraft from five- to sixty-five-seat capacity. ZK-MCM Piper PA31-350 Navajo Chieftain (c/n 31-7652032) is at Auckland in April 1992. Note lack of 'ZK' prefix. (*R.O'B.*)

Above: **Mahfooz Aviation** is a Jeddah, Saudi Arabia-based carrier with its aircraft registered in the Gambia. C5-DMB Boeing 727-228 (c/n 20411) is basking in the Sharjah sunshine after being pushed out of the SAIF Aviation Services hangar in March 1997.

Above: Australian operator **Masling Commuter Services** was based at Cootamundra, N.S.W. It flew a mix of Beech and Embraer types. Seen at Melbourne–Essendon in November 1978 is Embraer 110P2 Bandeirante VH-MWV (c/n 110190). The company was bought by Jet Charter Airlines in 1981 under the name Wings Australia. (*R.O'B.*)

Below: **Motop Sich – Aviakompania** is a Ukraine carrier based at Zaporozhye. It flies both passengers and cargo in a fleet of mixed types. UR48975 Antonov AN-12 (c/n 1400101) is on a cargo run to Sharjah, U.A.E., in March 1997.

Below: **MAS Kargo** is the freight division of Malaysian Airlines, based at Kuala Lumpur. 9M-MHI Boeing 747-236B (c/n 22304) lands at Dubai in March 1997.

Above: One of the oddest sub-charters for I/T holiday flights must have been when a 707 came from the African country of Burkino Faso. XT-BBF Boeing 707-328C (c/n 19521) of **Naganagani** is at Manchester–Ringway in May 1989. The company suspended operations in 1992.

Above: **Northern Air Cargo** of Anchorage, Alaska, is one of the biggest operators of the DC-6 in the world with a fleet of thirteen. Cargo is flown on both scheduled and charter operations around Alaska and to the 'lower 48'. N867TA Douglas DC-6 (c/n 45202) is at base in July 1992. (*R.O'B.*)

Below: **Northern Wilderness Outfitters Ltd** must be one of the best air transport names, even though it sounds like a shop for lumberjacks. C-GUTL de Havilland (Canada) DHC3 Otter (c/n 365), its Pratt & Whitney R1340 radial piston engine turning, moves across to the company base on Rainy Lake, Ontario, in June 1990. The airline flies fishermen and hunters to remote lakes.

Below: Based in Yellowknife, **Northwest Territorial Airways** flies scheduled passenger and cargo services around this far north and remote area of Canada. C-GNWC Lockheed L-188CF Electra (c/n 2015) is at Toronto in July 1986 operating a regular nightly cargo service.

Below: General cargo carrier **North East Bolivian Airways** is based at Cochabamba and has a fleet of two aircraft. CP1616 Curtiss C-46F Commando (c/n 22501) is at base in November 1992 in the very smart livery of the company.

Above: The Detroit-based **Nomads** is a travel club which currently operates a 727. From 1971 to 1981 it flew N836E Lockheed L-188C Electra (c/n 2008). It is seen on the ramp at Marana, Arizona, in October 1979.

Above: Stockholm-based **Nordic East** was founded in 1991 and flies Swedish holiday-makers on charters to the sun. The aircraft is used by other holiday companies. SE-DPX Lockheed L-1011 TriStar 1 (c/n 1091) arrives at Manchester–Ringway in September 1996 at the end of a charter.

Above: New York Air was one of the low-cost, high-frequency operators spawned by the deregulation of the American airline industry. N17317 Boeing 737-3T0 (c/n 23368) is at Boston in August 1986. The La Guardia-based airline was owned by the Texas Air Corporation which merged them into Continental Airlines the following year.

Below: Seen at Moscow–Bykovo in August 1995 is **Nadym Airlines** Yakovlev YAK-40K RA21505 (c/n 9830159). The carrier is from the town of Nadym in the Tyumen region of Russia. The operator has since been taken over by Gaspromavia.

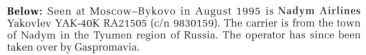

Below: Miami-based **National Airlines** had a history going back as far as 1934. In 1958, it was the first airline to use jets on domestic services in the U.S.A., using a leased Pan Am 707. It was Pan Am which took over National in 1980. N81NA Douglas DC-10-30 (c/n 46712) is at London–Heathrow in June 1978.

Above: Northwest Airlines of Minneapolis/St Paul, Minnesota, is one of America's giant carriers with services both domestic and international. N226NW Douglas DC-10-30 (c/n 46583) lands at London–Gatwick in June 1995 in the airline's current livery.

Below: Northwest Airlink is the commuter arm of the main operator feeding passengers to the giant twin cities (M.S.P.) hub. N271FA Fokker F27 Friendship 500 (c/n 10434) departs base in August 1986. The livery was the then current one. Note the name Northwest Orient; this stems from the fact that the carrier had a lot of services to the area. The word 'orient' has since been dropped.

Above: Northwest Cargo Boeing 747-251F N616US (c/n 21120) lands at New York–J.F.K. in May 1989 showing a very sparse livery.

Above: Canadian charter operator **Nationair** was based in French-speaking Montreal. C-GMXY Douglas DC-8-62 (c/n 45920) is at Toronto in July 1986. The airline was placed into receivership in March 1993 with suspension of services the following month.

Above: Same name but different company: Douglas DC-3 Dakota N600NA (c/n 3291) of **National Air Charters** at Sanford, Florida, in April 1994. This company, formed in 1993, operates just one aircraft for ad hoc passenger charter and pleasure flying. It is based at Daytona Beach.

Below: In the colours of **National Air Charters** N7043U Douglas DC-8-63F (c/n 46042) lands at New York–J.F.K. in May 1989. The stretched DC-8 has been a favourite with cargo operators for many years.

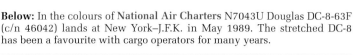

Above: **NFD** (Nurnberger Flugdienst) is a German international commuter line. D-ANFC Aérospatiale ATR 72-202 (c/n 237) arrives at London–Gatwick in August 1993. The new name Eurowings has since been adopted.

Below: Stavanger–based (then Oslo-based) **Norway Airlines** flew two 737s on charter work. LN-NOS Boeing 737-33A (c/n 23830) is at London–Gatwick in July 1988. The company suspended services in October 1992 but intends to restart services at some future date.

Below: **Nor-Fly Charter** of Oslo flew three Convairs on passenger charters carrying, for example, ships' crews. LN-BWG Convair CV-580 (c/n 42) is at Liverpool–Speke in April 1984 bringing in a football team. In January of the following year it merged into Partnair.

Above: **Nationwide Air** of Lanseria, South Africa, flies a mixed fleet of Beechcraft and BAC 111s for general charter work. ZS-NMT BAC 111-518FG (c/n 201) is at Durban in July 1996. (*R.O'B.*)

Above: With a very patriotic name and colour scheme **North American Airlines** Boeing 757-23A N757NA (c/n 24567) lands at Miami in April 1994. The company is based at New York–J.F.K. and flies charters.

Right: Owned by the government, **Nigeria Airways** flies across Africa as well as to Europe, America and the Middle East. SE-DFZ Boeing 747-283B (c/n 21575) climbs out of London–Heathrow in September 1986. The Swedish registration is due to the aircraft being on lease from S.A.S. (*S.G.W.*)

Above: **Nordair** flew scheduled passenger and cargo around the surrounding Canadian provinces from its base in Quebec. Charters are flown as far south as Florida and as far north as the D.E.W. Line defence chain on re-supply flights. C-GNDR Boeing 737-242 (c/n 22075) is at Toronto in July 1986. The following year it was merged into Canadian Pacific.

Below: **Norcanair** (North Canada Air) is based in the province of Saskatchewan flying both passengers and cargo on scheduled services to many local towns. C-GTEO Fokker F28 Fellowship 1000 (c/n 11991) is seen at the U.S. end of a daily service to Minneapolis/St Paul in July 1986. At the start of 1988 the company was merged into Time Air.

Above: **North Central Airlines** from its base in Minneapolis flew scheduled services across the surrounding states. N942V Douglas DC-9-32 (c/n 47459) is at New York–La Guardia in June 1976. Following a merger with Southern Airlines in 1979, Republic was formed. (*R.O'B.*)

Right: **Novair International Airways** used to be Calair; contrast the livery. It flew holiday charter work, both long- and short-haul. G-BJZD Douglas DC-10-10 (c/n 46970) is at Manchester–Ringway in May 1989. Operations ceased in May 1990. (*P.E.P.*)

Below: From the company base in North Bay, Ontario, **NorOntair** flew commuter services around the province. C-GGVX de Havilland (Canada) DHC6 Twin Otter 300 (c/n 462) is at Red Lake airport in June 1990. The carrier suspended operations in March 1996.

Below: Painted in the livery of **Necon Air** of Kathmandu, Nepal, this Avro (HS) 748-2B G-BKAL (c/n 1791) is seen landing at Manchester–Ringway in April 1995. The aeroplane was not delivered to them. (*J.D.S.*)

Above: North Star Air Cargo flies the stubby Shorts SC7 Skyvan 200 from its Anchorage, Alaska, location around the state. N51NS (c/n SH1843) is at base in July 1991. (*R.O'B.*)

Above: Nigerian airline **Okada Air** has been building up a fleet of twenty BAC 111s making it one of the biggest current users. At the larger end of the scale 5N-EDO Boeing 747-146 (c/n 19726) is serviced by F.L.S. at Manchester–Ringway in March 1994.

Below: Orion Airways of East Midlands–Castle Donington, U.K., was set up by Horizon Travel to fly its clients and for other charter work around Europe. G-BLKC Boeing 737-3T5 (c/n 23061) is at base in June 1988. The company was bought by Thomson Holidays and integrated into its airline, Britannia Airways, the following year.

Below: National Jet Systems of Adelaide, South Australia, flies a mix of passenger and freight aircraft. VH-NJQ BAe 146-200 (c/n E2176) is at base, July 1992. (*R.O'B.*)

Below: Olympic Airways is the Greek national airline with flights worldwide. SX-OAE Boeing 747-212B (c/n 21935) arrives back at the operator's Athens base in June 1993.

Above: Orion Air of Raleigh-Durham, North Carolina, was in the main concerned with cargo operations, providing handling services for small package carriers. One aircraft was used for passenger charters. N751PA Boeing 747-121 (c/n 19655) is about to depart Manchester–Ringway with a load of happy holidaymakers in July 1989. At the end of January 1990 operations were suspended.

Above: Looking after Greek commuter services is **Olympic Aviation**. Owned by Olympic Airways it has a network of scheduled services to the many Greek islands as well as mainland towns. SX-BHC Dornier DO228-201 (c/n 8030) lands at Athens, June 1993.

Right: Odyssey International was a short-lived Canadian charter operation. C-GAWB Boeing 757-28A (c/n 24367) is at Manchester–Ringway in July 1990. The company started in 1988 and closed in 1990.

Above: Oasis International Airlines is a Spanish holiday charter operator based at Palma, Majorca. EC-FVC McDonnell Douglas MD-83 (c/n 49629) arrives at Liverpool–Speke in May 1995. In 1996 the company filed for the Spanish equivalent of Chapter 11 and was expected to cease services.

Below: Ozark Air Lines was founded in 1946 in St Louis, Missouri. It grew to be a large domestic carrier flying to many parts of the country with a large fleet of DC-9s. N970Z Douglas DC-9-15 (c/n 45772) lands at Miami in October 1981. The company was taken over by T.W.A. in 1986.

Above: ONA – Overseas National Airways – was formed in 1950 and specialised in contracts to the U.S. military. N938F Douglas DC-9-32F (c/n 47221) is on the ramp at Norfolk Naval Air Station, May 1972. This aeroplane was eventually sold to the U.S. Navy. The airline suspended operations in September 1978. (*S.G.W.*)

Above: Onur Air of Istanbul is owned by two Turkish holiday companies which use the airline to fly their clients. TC-ONG Airbus A320-211 (c/n 361) arrives at Manchester–Ringway in June 1996.

Below: Russian operator Orenburg Airlines is based in the city of that name. RA85595 Tupolev TU-154B2 (c/n 595) awaits the next passenger load at Moscow–Domodedovo in August 1995. Note the colour scheme is similar to the old Aeroflot.

Below: Started in 1994, Orient Avia is a Russian airline flying from Moscow to the far east of that country. RA86567 Ilyushin IL-62M (c/n 4256314) is at the company base of Sheremetyevo in September 1995.

Below: OLT (Ostfriesische Lufttransport) is based in Emden and flies commuter air taxi operations. D-FOLE Cessna 208B Caravan (c/n 0523) is at Düsseldorf in July 1996. Note it is in passenger configuration; most Caravans fly cargo. (*P.E.P.*)

Above: Aeroflot never looked this good. Showing one of the better liveries to be seen in Russia today is **Orel Avia** Yakovlev YAK-42D RA42434 (c/n 4520424305017) at Moscow–Sheremetyevo in August 1995. The airline is based in the town of Lipetsk. (*J.D.S.*)

Below: **Paramount Airways** was a British holiday charter operator based in Bristol. G-PATA McDonnell Douglas MD-83 (c/n 49398) is about to turn on to the runway at Liverpool–Speke in April 1989. The following year operations ceased. (*P.E.P.*)

Above: **Oman Air** is the carrier based in Muscat in the Sultanate of Oman. A40-MB Airbus A320-231 (c/n 225) arrives on a scheduled passenger flight at Dubai, U.A.E., in March 1997. (*J.D.S.*)

Below: **PSA** (Pacific Southwest Airlines) was based in San Diego, California. It offered high frequency and low fares along the Pacific coast and into the western states. N545PS Boeing 727-214 (c/n 20169) is at San Francisco–S.F.O. in October 1979. The carrier was merged into U.S. Air during 1988.

Above: Lisbon-based airline **Portugalia** flies a fleet of six Fokkers. Seen at Manchester–Ringway in June 1996, on a football charter, is CS-TPF Fokker 100 (c/n 11258).

Above: **PBA** (Provincetown Boston Airlines) was based at Hyannis, Massachusetts, and Naples, Florida. After services in the summer in Massachusetts they would head south and fly winter services in sunny Florida. N43PB Douglas DC-3A Dakota (c/n 1953) is on the move at Boston in August 1986. The airline was taken over by Bar Harbor in September 1988.

Right: Powell Air of Powell River, British Columbia, is like many Canadian bush operators flying aircraft on a mix of wheels/floats/skis depending on location and season. C-FXUY de Havilland (Canada) DHC3 Otter (c/n 142) is at Vancouver airport S.P.B. in September 1984. During 1988 the airline merged with Pacific Coastal Airlines.

Above: Polaris Air Transport of Oslo had this Convair in store at Woensdrecht, Holland, in July 1970, LN-KLT Convair CV240 (c/n 310). The carrier had operated a fleet of three CV-240s and two Dakotas between 1966 and 1969 when operations were suspended.

Below: Scottish-based **Peregrine Air Services** flew commuter and air taxi services. G-BKHI BAe 3102 Jetstream 31 (c/n 604) is on a scheduled service to Manchester–Ringway in September 1984. The name was changed to Aberdeen Airways in 1989.

Above: Turkish charter airline **Pegasus** is an example of international co-operation as it is a subsidiary of Aer Lingus. TC-AFK Boeing 737-4Y0 (c/n 24684) is seen departing Liverpool–Speke in May 1995 with a full load of sunseekers.

Above: Philippine Airlines is the national airline with services both domestic and worldwide. PI-C-1021 Avro (HS) 748 Srs 2-209 (c/n 1642) is in the manufacturer's flight sheds at Woodford, June 1968. Note the registration prefix 'PI'; this changed to the current 'RP' in 1974.

Below: Danish charter airline **Premiair** is the result of an amalgamation of Conair and Sweden's Scanair. SE-DHS Douglas DC-10-10 (c/n 46646) arrives at Manchester–Ringway in June 1996 on a football charter.

Below: PointAir (Le Point Air Sarl) was a French airline formed in 1981 for long-haul charters. F-BSGT Boeing 707-321B (c/n 18837) is at Stansted, U.K., in August 1985. The Lyon-based operator suspended services in 1987. (*J.D.S.*)

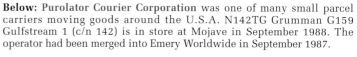

Below: Purolator Courier Corporation was one of many small parcel carriers moving goods around the U.S.A. N142TG Grumman G159 Gulfstream 1 (c/n 142) is in store at Mojave in September 1988. The operator had been merged into Emery Worldwide in September 1987.

Above: Edmonton, Canada-based **Points of Call** flew just one aircraft. C-FNZE Douglas DC8-52 (c/n 45985) is at Hamilton, Ontario, in June 1990. The airline had suspended services six months earlier.

Below: Polar Air Cargo is an all-747 operator based at New York–J.F.K. airport. N855FT Boeing 747-124F (c/n 19733) is at Moscow–Sheremetyevo in September 1995.

Above: Pan West is a good, typical name for an airline. Film-makers thought so and we have the result. 'N375' Convair CV880-22-1 at Mojave, California, in September 1988. Both the airline and the registration are fictional, having been painted for a T.V. series in 1986 called *Amazing Stories*. The real identity of the aircraft is N814AJ (c/n 32).

Below: Pacific Western Airlines of Vancouver, British Columbia, operated an extensive route network of scheduled passenger flights around the western provinces of Canada and into the U.S.A. C-GUPW Boeing 737-275 (c/n 22873) is at Toronto in July 1986. The airline was merged into Canadian in April 1987.

Above: Flying commuter services from its Winnipeg, Manitoba, base, **Perimeter** services some very remote locations. C-GCRA Fairchild F27J (c/n 52) is at base, June 1990.

Above: American east-coast operator **Presidential Airways** started up in 1985 to give high-frequency/low-fare flights with a full service. N304XV Boeing 737-230C (c/n 20256) is at Boston, August 1986. Operations were suspended in December 1989.

Right: Pan American World Airways, from its formation in 1927, grew to be perhaps the best known airline in the world. N814PA Airbus A310-324 (c/n 450) is landing at the company base of New York–J.F.K. in May 1989. The airline was hit by competition more and more and the great name ceased trading in December 1991. In 1996 a new company has acquired the name of Pan Am and resumed services.

Above: PLUNA (Primeras Lineas Uruguayas de Navegación Aerea) is the national airline of Uruguay. Most services are concentrated around South America. CX-BOO Boeing 737-2A3 (c/n 22738) is at Buenos Aires Aeroparque, November 1995. (R.O'B.)

Below: Miami-based **Pan Aviation** flew a mix of cargo and executive aircraft. N722GS Boeing 707-321C (c/n 19377) is at base, August 1986. During 1992 flying operations were suspended and the company now acts as a broker.

Above: Honolulu-based **Pacific Air Express** operated a freight service around the Hawaiian islands until operations were suspended in August 1986. N301JT Douglas DC-4 Skymaster (c/n 18375) is seen at Chandler, Arizona, in store during September 1988.

Above: **Precision Airways** was based in Manchester, New Hampshire, and flew commuter services around New England. N55RP Beechcraft C99 Commuter (c/n U-198) arrives at Albany, New York, in July 1986. The operator became a Northwest Airlink company but went out of service in January 1995.

Below: Puerto Rico-based **Prinair** was the last large user of the Heron. N587PR de Havilland DH114 Heron 2D (c/n 14148) is at San Juan in November 1992. Operations had ceased in 1985.

Below: The rise and fall of **People Express** is now a subject in business school. The carrier was formed in 1980 and grew at such a rate it was not able to handle the volume of passenger that flocked to the Newark, New Jersey, base. N605PE Boeing 747-243B (c/n 20520) is at London–Gatwick in July 1986. Continental Airlines took over the airline in February 1987.

Below: Phoenix was a Swiss charter line, based in Basle, which started services in the spring of 1971. HB-IEG Boeing 707-131 (c/n 17671) is at Zürich, June 1973. Operations were terminated in the spring of 1974. (*J.D.S.*)

Above: Pan Am Express was the commuter arm of the main company. Unlike the parent it was based in Philadelphia. N175RA de Havilland (Canada) DHC7-102 Dash 7 (c/n 56) lands at New York–J.F.K. in May 1989. It also ceased operations in 1991.

Below: Paradise Island Airlines flies from Florida to the Bahamas. N780MG de Havilland (Canada) DHC7 Dash 7-102 (c/n 80) is landing at Miami in June 1989. The company at that time was part of Chalks, Resorts International was the next owner, and currently it flies as a U.S. Air Express carrier.

Above: Polynesian Airline of Samoa is a government-owned carrier based in the capital of Western Samoa, Apia. Services both passenger and cargo are flown over a wide area. 5W-ILF Boeing 737-3Q8 (c/n 26282) is at Melbourne–Tullamarine, October 1996. (*R.O'B.*)

Below: Progressive Airways was a Norwich, U.K.-based independent that evolved from Tyler Aviation. The airline was launched in November 1970 with a plan to start scheduled passenger services the following January. G-AYTW Vickers Viscount 803 (c/n 175) is at Dublin, July 1971. The carrier had folded in April of that year and the Viscount, an ex-Aer Lingus example, was never delivered. (*S.G.W.*)

Above: Pakistan International Airlines – PIA – is the government-owned flag carrier based at Karachi. AP-BEB Airbus A310-308 (c/n 587) lands at Athens, June 1993.

Above: From its formation in 1948, North Carolina-based **Piedmont Airlines** grew to have a fleet of over 200 airliners. N247P NAMC YS 11A-205 (c/n 2114) is at Atlanta in July 1974. Early in 1989 the company became USAir. (*S.G.W.*)

Right: Operating the company's cargo services is **PIA Cargo**. AP-BBK Boeing 707-323C (c/n 19576) is at Athens, June 1993.

Above: Pegasus Travel had Rich International paint the aeroplane it leased for passenger charters in its colours. N1805 Douglas DC-8-62 (c/n 45899) is at Miami in June 1989.

Above: Russian operator **Permtransavia** is part of Perm Motors, flying corporate services as well as normal cargo and passenger charters. RA65983 Tupolev TU-134A is seen at Sharjah in March 1997.

Below: Polet (Rossijskaya Aviakompania) is a Russian passenger/cargo carrier. RA11325 Antonov AN-12 (c/n 5342801) is at Sharjah, U.A.E., in March 1997 on a cargo service.

Above: New Iranian operator **Payan Air** flies this Ilyushin IL-76M EP-TPZ (c/n 073410284) on cargo services. It is seen arriving at Sharjah in March 1997, in the early evening sunshine.

Above: Flying the commuters was **Piedmont Commuter System**. Like most such operations the airline was independent and flew in the major's livery and used its flight numbers. N102UR Swearingen SA226 Metro II (c/n TC-251) departs Dayton, Ohio, in July 1986. The aircraft is owned by Britt Airways.

Below: QANTAS gets its name from Queensland and Northern Territory Aerial Services. It is Australia's flag carrier and operates services worldwide. VH-OJK Boeing 747-438 (c/n 25067) is at Manchester–Ringway in May 1992.

Below: Canadian airline **Quebecair** provided scheduled passenger flights around the province, to other Canadian cities, and into the eastern states of America. C-GQBB Boeing 737-296 (c/n 22276) is at Toronto in July 1986. The carrier later became part of Canadian.

Above: Qatar Airways is based in the capital, Doha. It flies both long- and short-haul passenger services with three 727s and three 747s. A7-ABC Boeing 727-2M7 (c/n 21951) lands at Dubai in March 1997.

Below: Republic Airlines was the name picked following the merger of North Central Airlines and Southern Airways in 1979. The new company was based in the former's site at Minneapolis/St Paul. N963N Douglas DC-9-31 (c/n 47415) lands at Miami in October 1981. The company were taken over by the other Minneapolis-based airline, Northwest, in 1986.

Below: Rutaca (Rutas Aereas) is a Venezuelan general service operator flying cargo and passengers with a variety of types. YV222C Douglas DC-3 Dakota (c/n 7386) is at the company base of Ciudad Bolivar in November 1992.

Above: Looking after the airline's commuters was **Republic Express**. It was a franchise operation by Express Airlines and painted in Republic colours. N324PX Saab SF340A (c/n 048) is at the company base, Minneapolis, July 1986.

Below: British cargo airline **Redcoat** was based at Luton. With three Britannias and a CL44, charters were flown around the U.K., Europe and Africa. Canadair CL44D-4-2 G-BRED (c/n 37) is in store at Luton, September 1983. In May of the previous year the company had ceased trading and became bankrupt.

Above: RAS (Rijnmond Air Services) is a Rotterdam-based small parcel-passenger carrier. PH-RAZ Swearingen SA226TC Metro II (c/n TC-252) is seen at Liverpool–Speke in June 1996 having brought in football supporters.

Above: RAS (Rheinland Air Service) is a German commuter line with a fleet of four aircraft. D-CBAS Short SD360-300 (c/n SH3764) is at the airline's Düsseldorf base in May 1995. (*P.E.P.*)

Right: When Rich International Airways started services in 1971 it flew Curtiss C-46s on cargo flights from its Miami base. The airline grew to be a major passenger charter company with seventeen jet airliners, thirteen of which are TriStars. N305GB Lockheed L-1011 TriStar 1 (c/n 1127) is at Manchester–Ringway in May 1996. November of that year saw the company file for Chapter 11 and suspend operations with the intention of a quick restart in early 1997.

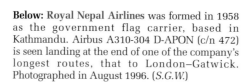

Above: With the morning sun glinting off the aircraft, C-GEHX Beech 18 (c/n CA 112) of **Red Lake Airways** departs the company base of Red Lake, Ontario, for a charter flight in June 1990. The carrier is an all-float operator flying tourists from May to October.

Below: Royal Nepal Airlines was formed in 1958 as the government flag carrier, based in Kathmandu. Airbus A310-304 D-APON (c/n 472) is seen landing at the end of one of the company's longest routes, that to London–Gatwick. Photographed in August 1996. (*S.G.W.*)

Above: Seen here at Tucson, Arizona, in October 1984 is Vickers Viscount 786D XA-MOS (c/n 334) still in the colours of Mexico City-based **Republica**. The airline had used the aircraft on lease from its owner the Go Group. During 1985 the airline ceased operations.

Above: German commuter line **RFG** – Regional Flug – was a Dortmund-based passenger carrier with domestic and international services. D-BCRS Aérospatiale ATR 42-300 (c/n 287) is seen at London–Gatwick in August 1993. The aircraft was awaiting a repaint. As of 1 January of that year the airline merged into Eurowings.

Below: Reed Aviation has its colours on this Emerald Airways 748. The aircraft in freight configuration carries the Reed name. G-ATMI Avro (HS) 748 Srs 2A-225 (c/n 1592) is at home base of Liverpool–Speke in June 1994.

Below: RIAir, Riga Airlines of Latvia, has leased this 737 from Russian carrier Transaero; it is the airline's total fleet. YL-BAB Boeing 737-236 (c/n 22032) is at Moscow–Sheremetyevo 1 in September 1995.

Above: Locations such as Alaska and its Aleutian Island chain could not function the way they do without an airline like **Reeve Aleutian**. From its base in Anchorage it flies both passengers and cargo around the region. N171RV NAMC YS 11A-307 (c/n 2071) is seen at base in July 1979. (*R.O'B.*)

Above: Yorkshire Television in Britain made a series in 1981/2 called *Airline*, the story of a fictional company, **Ruskin Air Services**, from its formation just after World War Two onwards. A real Douglas DC-3 Dakota was supplied by Aces High (G-DAKS c/n 19347) and painted with a period registration of 'G-AGHY'. It is seen at an airshow at Mildenhall in May 1982.

Below: **Royal Air Cambodge** flies from the capital of Cambodia, Phnom-Penh. The airline was formed in 1994 and leases the equipment. 9M-MJT Boeing 737-4Y0 (c/n 24915) is at Bangkok in February 1996. The aircraft is on lease from Malaysian, hence the registration. (*J.D.S.*)

Below: **Royal Air Maroc** (RAM) is the government-owned airline of Morocco based in Casablanca. The carrier flies services to North Africa, Europe, the Middle East and America. CN-RMP Boeing 727-2B6 (c/n 21298) is seen landing at Athens in June 1993.

Below: Irish airline **Ryanair** has grown by offering low-price, no-frills services from the company base in Dublin. EI-CKS Boeing 737-2T5 (c/n 22023) arrives at Liverpool–Speke on a scheduled service from Dublin in October 1996. (See Special Colour Schemes, p. 142.)

Above: **Royal Jordanian**, based in the capital, Amman, is the country's flag carrier. F-ODVI Airbus A310-304 (c/n 531) lands at Athens in June 1993. The distinctive and attractive colour scheme does need full sunlight to be seen to full effect.

Above: **Roadway Global Air** was the aviation arm of a trucking operation. N110NE Boeing 727-81F (c/n 18952) is at Fort Lauderdale in April 1994. The carrier suspended operations in November 1995.

Right: The visit in June 1993 of a Latvian aircraft to Liverpool–Speke was very much a first. YL-RAC Antonov AN-26 (c/n 9903) of **RAF-AVIA** had brought in a ship's crew.

Above: **Reliant Airlines** of Detroit–Willow Run has a fleet of nine Falcons in freight configuration to fly motor industry components and general cargo around the country. N212R Dassault Falcon 20DC (c/n 212) is at base, July 1986.

Above: **Royal Aviation** is a Montreal-based charter line for passenger flights. C-FTNI Lockheed L-1011 TriStar 100 (c/n 1058) is on the move at London–Gatwick in August 1995. (*S.G.W.*)

Below: Seen at Los Angeles–LAX in October 1995 is **Reno Air** McDonnell Douglas MD-82 N824RA (c/n 53017). The Nevada-based company flies a fleet of twenty-seven jet airliners. (*S.G.W.*)

Above: Bremen-based **ROA** (Roland Air, Flugverkehr & Vertriebs) has a fleet of five Metros. D-IHCW Swearingen SA226TC Metro II (c/n TC 350) is at Düsseldorf in May 1995. The airline is owned by OLT (*P.E.P.*)

Above: **Rusty Myer's Flying Services** is based at Fort Francis S.P.B. It flies fishermen and hunters to cabins on the many lakes in the area. C-FERM Beech 18 (c/n CA 62), with shark's mouth nose art, poses for the camera over the carrier's northern Ontario base in June 1990. The camera ship was another Beech 18 of the airline.

Below: **Regional Airlines** of Nantes in France flies commuters around western Europe. F-GHVT Saab SF340B (c/n 340B-276) is on a service to Düsseldorf in May 1995. (*P.E.P.*)

Below: **Royal Swazi National Airlines** has two aircraft in the fleet, both Fokkers. 3D-ALN Fokker F28 Fellowship 3000 (c/n 11136) is at Nairobi in August 1980 on a flight from the Swaziland capital of Manzini. (*R.O'B.*)

Above: Red Carpet Airlines was a general charter operator based at St Petersburg, Florida. N902RC Convair CV-440 (c/n 118) is at Nassau in the Bahamas in August 1980. The carrier had a name change and became Aerosun International in August 1991. (*R.O'B.*)

Below: Rio-Sul (Servicios Aereos Regionais) is a Brazilian domestic airline owned by Varig. PT-SLF Embraer 120RT Brasilia (c/n 120043) is at the company base of Rio de Janeiro in January 1992. (*R.O'B.*)

Above: Royal Brunei Airlines has this most attractive yellow colour scheme. V8-RBG Boeing 767-33A (c/n 25532) lines up to land on runway 09L at London–Heathrow in September 1993. The Sultan of Brunei, a very rich oil producer, has a couple of his fleet of large executive jets in the airline livery.

Below: British independent airline South-West Aviation was based at Exeter and from its formation in 1966 flew charters of an ad hoc variety. Contract flying included fruit and flowers from the Channel Islands. G-AMYJ Douglas DC-3 Dakota (c/n 32716) is at base in August 1970. In October 1972 the company was bought out and moved.

Below: Turkish charter line **Sunways Intersun Havacilik** has a fleet of four MD-83s. TC-IND McDonnell Douglas MD-83 (c/n 49940) is about to turn on to the runway at Liverpool–Speke, August 1996, on a holiday charter flight to the Turkish coast.

Above: American commuter airline **Swift Aire** began operations in March 1969; it grew to have a fleet of Fokker F27 Friendships, operating over 100 daily departures between points in California. N414SA de Havilland DH114 Heron 2B (c/n 14056) is at the company base of San Luis Obispo in October 1979. The carrier ceased services in September 1981.

Above: New Russian carrier **Samara Airlines** has kept the basic old Aeroflot scheme with just a name and logo added. RA85-500 Tupolev TU-154B-2 (c/n 500) is at Moscow–Domodedovo in August 1995.

Right: Seagreen Air Transport of St John's, Antigua, had flown Dakotas since 1968. It operated scheduled cargo flights around the Leeward Islands and beyond. V2-LIX Douglas DC-3 Dakota (c/n 25623) is at base in June 1983. Note the Morris 1000 car under the wing. The carrier ceased services in 1985. (*R.O'B.*)

Above: Spanish charter line **Spantax** had a history dating back to 1959, flying services into most British airports. EC-BTE Convair CV990-30A-5 (c/n 21) is on the ramp at the company's Palma, Majorca, base in January 1972. The airline suspended services in March 1988. (*S.G.W.*)

Below: Seafood Resources International leased this Douglas DC-4 Skymaster N44909 (c/n 27371) from Biegert Aviation. The interior had been fitted out for the carriage of fish. The aircraft is at Chandler, Arizona, in October 1984.

Above: Santa Cruz Imperial is a Sharjah, U.A.E.-based all-cargo carrier founded in 1996. The fleet is registered in either Liberia or Djibouti. EL-AKZ Antonov AN-8 is at base in March 1997. The AN-8 is a very rare aircraft that was once thought to be extinct. Six were to be seen at Sharjah!

Above: Sunbelt Airlines was an Arkansas-based commuter and air taxi company. N913SB Shorts SD360-100 (c/n SH3629) is in store at Marana, Arizona, in October 1984, the airline having suspended services that month.

Below: Minneapolis-based **Sun Country Airlines** is an American charter line founded by ex-Braniff staff. N102UA Douglas DC-10-10 (c/n 46905) is at Miami, April 1994.

Below: Sky Pak International Couriers is a marketing name of TNT. G-TJPM BAe 146-300QT (c/n E3150) is at Liverpool–Speke in May 1995. The aircraft awaits its overnight cargo load.

Above: **Spirit Airlines** is a Detroit, Michigan-based passenger line, with up to 30% of the carrier's work in the form of charters. N932ML Douglas DC-9-31 (c/n 47547) is at Orlando, Florida, in April 1994.

Below: **Sudan Airways** is the government-owned airline based in Khartoum. It flies around Africa, the Middle East and Europe. F-OGQN Airbus A310-304 (c/n 418) lands at London–Heathrow in July 1995.

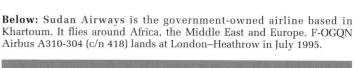

Below: Tucson-based **Sierra Pacific Airlines** has been flying passengers around the western states since 1976. N73153 Convair CV-580 (c/n 179) is receiving maintenance at Marana, Arizona, in October 1984.

Above: The national airline of Belgium is **SABENA** (Société Anonyme Belge d'Exploitation de la Navigation Aérienne), with a history dating back to 1923. The company flies services worldwide from its Brussels base. OO-SYA Boeing 737-329 (c/n 24355) lands at London–Heathrow in July 1995.

Below: **Spanair** is a Palma, Majorca-based holiday charter operator with a fleet of MD-83s and 767s. EC-FHA Boeing 767-3Y0 (c/n 25000) is pushed back from Terminal 1 at Manchester–Ringway in June 1996.

Above: **Singapore Airlines** (SIA) was formed in 1972 and flies services worldwide. It claims to have the best cabin service and the newest fleet. 9V-SMZ Boeing 747-412 (c/n 26549) lands at Manchester–Ringway in August 1995.

Above: **Saudia** – Saudi Arabian Airlines is the government-owned flag carrier, with services flown worldwide. HZ-AHC Lockheed L-1011 TriStar 100 (c/n 1137) is at Paris–Charles de Gaulle in May 1977.

Right: Syrian Arab Airlines (Syrianair) is the only airline in that country. It flies passengers and freight on domestic and international services. YK-AFD Sud Aviation SE210 Caravelle 10B-3 (c/n 186) lands at Athens in June 1993 with smoke pouring out of the two Pratt & Whitney JT8D jets. These levels of smoke are one of the reasons that the SE210 is now not very common.

Above: U.K.-based Suckling Airways fly scheduled services, both domestic and international, from its Cambridge base. G-BVPT Dornier Do228-202K (c/n 8165) lands at Manchester–Ringway in June 1996.

Below: Sabourin Lake Airways is based at Cochenour, Ontario, Canada. It flies a mixture of land and float operations. C-GPHD de Havilland (Canada) DHC3 Otter (c/n 113) is on the move on Sabourin Lake in June 1990.

Above: French charter line Star Europe (Société de Transport Aérien Regional) flies from Paris–Orly. F-GRSB Boeing 737-497 (c/n 25663) is at London–Gatwick in August 1996. (*S.G.W.*)

Above: Skycraft Air Transport of Oshawa, Ontario, was a mixed-service Canadian operator flying passenger charters, freight and commuters. C-GHOY Embraer 110P1 Bandeirante (c/n 110277) is at base in July 1986. The airline suspended operations in February 1994.

Below: SMB Stage Line (Sedalia Marshall Boonville) were a Dallas–D.F.W.-based freight carrier with a large fleet of Convairs. N94246 Convair CV-600 (c/n 102) is waiting its next cargo at Richmond, Virginia, in May 1989. The following year the airline closed down.

Below: Skywest is a large American commuter line flying in the western states. It flies three types of aircraft: Metros, Brasilias and Regional Jets. N189SW Embraer EMB120 Brasilia (c/n 120048) lands at Reno Cannon, Nevada, in September 1988. The airline can be found operating as a Delta Connection company.

Above: **Sterling Airways** of Copenhagen has since 1962 flown holidaymakers around European sunspots and beyond. OY-SAT Boeing 727-2J4 (c/n 20766) arrives at Athens in June 1993. Three months later the airline suspended services only to be reborn as Sterling European Airways.

Below: Flying services from Detroit–Willow Run is **SkyWay Enterprises**. The airline flies small freight or passengers on charter operations. N48BA Learjet 24 (c/n 24-152) is at base, June 1990.

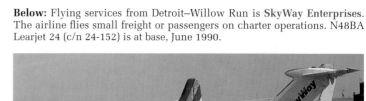

Below: Danish carrier **Star Air** flies freight most of the time. OY-SRR Fokker F27 Friendship 600 (c/n 10392) is at Manchester–Ringway in July 1989. This aircraft is used for both passengers and freight. The blue colour scheme reveals the fact that it is an associate company of Maersk.

Above: **Sioux Air** is a small Canadian back-woods operator flying tourists who want to get away from it all. C-FHEP de Havilland (Canada) DHC2 Beaver (c/n 69) taxies into dock at the company base of Sioux Lookout, Ontario, in June 1990. The 'Knobby' title relates to the company owner Mr Glen 'Knobby' Clark.

Below: **ScanBee** (Scandinavian Beeline Charter) was a Swedish charter company with a single Convair. N14CD Convair CV-340 (c/n 99) is seen at Fort Lauderdale in October 1981 after it had been replaced by a turboprop CV-580. The airline continued services until 1986.

Above: **Skyjet** is based in both Brussels and Antigua. It leases out its aircraft to airlines for short terms. V2-LEA Douglas DC-10-30 (c/n 46554) is at London–Gatwick in August 1993.

Above: British commuter operator **Streamline Aviation** was based at East Midlands–Castle Donington. G-OPPP Embraer 110P1 Bandeirante (c/n 110235) is at base, July 1991. The company has since moved to Exeter in the south-west of England.

Below: Based in Seattle, Washington, **Salair** flies cargo on an ad hoc and charter basis. Seen at Sacramento Municipal, California, in October 1984 is N107AD Douglas DC-3 Dakota (c/n 12438) being loaded with cargo.

Below: Surinam is the old Dutch Guiana on the South American mainland. Based in the capital of Paramaribo is **Surinam Airways** which flies around the region as well as running some domestic services; in conjunction with KLM a service is run to Amsterdam. N1809E Douglas DC-8-62 (c/n 46107) shows off its very bright colours at Miami in June 1989.

Above: **SAL South African Airlines** (the SAL stands for Suid Afrikaanse Lugdiens) is the government flag carrier with a history dating back to 1934. ZS-SPE Boeing 747SP-44 (c/n 21254) is at London–Heathrow in May 1988. The airline flies worldwide and has expanded service into Africa since the change of power in the country.

Above: **South Coast Airlines** was a small Australian air taxi operator based at Melbourne–Essendon. VH-IRB Cessna 414 (c/n 414-0425) shows off its colours, or rather lack of them, at base in December 1979. (*R.O'B.*)

Below: **SAS** – Scandinavian Airline System – is the multinational airline of Sweden, Norway and Denmark. Set up in 1946 it flies services worldwide. LN-RCC Boeing 767-283ER (c/n 24728) arrives at London–Heathrow in September 1993. Aircraft are registered using either LN, SE or OY. (See Special Colour Schemes, p. 142.)

Above: **South Coast Airways** of the U.K. is the operator of a single aircraft, used for pleasure flying and special charters. G-DAKK Douglas DC-3 Dakota (c/n 9798) is at an air show at Biggin Hill in June 1996. (*S.G.W.*)

Above: Las Vegas-based **Scenic Airways** flies tourists to many of the region's sights such as the Grand Canyon; normal commuter services also cover the area. N76GC Ford Trimotor 5-AT-C (c/n 5AT-11) is at base, October 1979.

Above: Sun D'Or International Airlines is a Tel Aviv-based subsidiary of El Al; it took its current name in 1981. 4X-ATY Boeing 707-358C (c/n 20301) is at Manchester–Ringway in June 1982. (*P.E.P.*)

Above: Simba Air Cargo is an air cargo operator based in the Kenyan capital of Nairobi. 5Y-SIM Boeing 707-336C (c/n 20517) is at Stansted, U.K., in May 1995. (*S.G.W.*)

Below: Serca (Servicio Especializado de Carga Aerea) of Bogota, Colombia, flies a mix of cargo and passengers. The latter can charter this executive fit Convair CV-580 HK3666 (c/n 18). It is seen on the ramp at Medellin in November 1992. The company now styles its name SEC Colombia.

Below: Sabre Airways is a Gatwick-based charter company. G-BPND Boeing 727-2D3 (c/n 21021) arrives at Manchester–Ringway's Terminal 2 in June 1996.

Below: Siller Bros Aviation of Yuba City, California, flies heavy helicopters on a multitude of tasks. N4035S Sikorsky S64 Skycrane (c/n 64099) is at Detroit–Willow Run in July 1986.

Above: Safair is a South African cargo charter company formed in 1969. The holding company is shipping company Safmarine. ZS-LSF Boeing 707-344C (c/n 20283) is on the ramp at Cape Town in May 1986. (*R.O'B.*)

Above: The rise of the Turkish tourism industry has seen a similar rise in charter airlines. **Sun Express** is based at Antalya. TC-SUS Boeing 737-430 (c/n 27007) is at Düsseldorf in May 1995. (*P.E.P.*)

117

Right: St Lucia Airways – SLA – was founded in 1974; most of the fleet were commuters for services around the West Indies. The one large aircraft was Boeing 707-323C J6-SLF (c/n 18689) seen departing London–Gatwick in May 1982 in its role as a freight carrier. Operations were suspended in 1987. (*P.E.P.*)

Above: Selva Colombia (Servicios Aereos del Vaupes) is a Villavicencio-based cargo operator flying anything, anywhere. HK3150 Curtiss C-46A Commando (c/n 26812) is at base, November 1992.

Below: Swissair is one of the world's best known airlines flying services on a worldwide basis. Boeing 747-357 HB-IGD (c/n 22705) departs the company H.Q. at Zürich on a wet day in August 1987.

Above: French cargo line SFAir was set up in 1980 to carry outsize cargo, livestock and relief supplies. F-GDAQ Lockheed L-100-30 (c/n 4600) is at Paris–Le Bourget in May 1983. The airline was taken over by Minerve in 1987 and renamed Jet Fret. (*J.D.S.*)

Above: Finland has produced few charter airlines; Spearair is one. OH-SOA Douglas DC-8-32 (c/n 45606) is seen in a very smart livery at London–Gatwick in August 1973. When the travel company that owned the airline went out of business in May 1974, the airline followed. (*J.D.S.*)

Below: SAM – Società Aerea Mediterranea – was a common sight at U.K. airports during the 1960s. The Rome-based company, owned by Alitalia, flew hundreds of charter flights. I-DIMD Douglas DC-6B (c/n 44419) is at London–Gatwick in August 1969. The airline was merged into the parent company in 1974. (*S.G.W.*)

Below: U.K. commuter line Spacegrand was based in the north-west town of Blackpool. G-BGMD de Havilland (Canada) DHC6 Twin Otter 310 (c/n 629) is seen at Liverpool–Speke in April 1983. The airline was merged into Jersey European in 1985.

Below: Skywest Aviation of Perth, Australia, is a multi-functional operation looking after such diverse tasks as coastal survey, photography, air ambulance and commuter flying. VH-WBI Embraer 110P2 Bandeirante (c/n 110292) is at base, May 1986. (*R.O'B.*)

Above: South East Air was a small British operator flying freight and post. It leased a Herald from Channel Express in 1987. G-CEAS Handley Page HPR7 Herald 214 (c/n 186) is at Stansted in August of that year. Early the following year services were suspended. (*J.D.S.*)

Below: From Oakland, California, Saturn Airways was a regular visitor to the U.K. on passenger charter flights. N3325T Douglas DC-8F-55 (c/n 45754) is at London–Gatwick in August 1969. Saturn merged its identity with TIA in December 1976. (*S.G.W.*)

Above: Iranian carrier Saha Airlines keeps a low profile with regard to its name. This jumbo has it in small letters under the nose. This may be due to the operator's alleged connections with the Iranian Air Force. EP-SHH Boeing 747-259F (c/n 21487) departs Sharjah in March 1997. The aircraft still carries an air force serial of (5-8)114.

Below: Southern Airways of Atlanta, Georgia, was formed in 1949 and grew to cover many states. N149S Martin 404 (c/n 14141) arrives at base in July 1974. The company merged with North Central to form Republic in 1979. (*S.G.W.*)

Above: Shawnee Airlines of Florida flew a variety of propliners from its start-up in 1968. As a subsidiary of Air Florida it flew scheduled passenger services around the state and across to the Bahamas. N258S Martin 404 (c/n 14232) is at Fort Lauderdale in August 1974. The carrier hit hard times and ceased operations in 1979. (*R.O'B.*)

Above: Sea & Sun Airlines is a wonderful name for a charter airline. New York-based, it leased two of its fleet of four to Los Angeles carrier Pacific East Air. N3931G Douglas DC-8-62H (c/n 45986) is at Marana in October 1984 with the marks of both airlines. Sun & Sea suspended services in 1985.

Below: British operator **Skyways Coach Air** was one of the first airlines to fly people on holiday. A coach took passengers to the airport, the aeroplane crossed the English Channel, and another coach took them to the city they were to stay in. G-ALZZ Airspeed AS57 Ambassador 2 (c/n 5222) is at London–Gatwick in August 1968. This aircraft was on a four-month lease from Autair. In 1972 the company was taken over by Dan Air.

Below: SAETA (Sociedad Anonima Ecuatoriana de Transportes Aereos) – Air Ecuador – is based in Quito. Scheduled services are flown to South/Central/North America. HC-BRG Boeing 727-282 (c/n 20973) is at Miami, November 1992.

Above: **Skyways Air Cargo** was part of the same holding group; based at Lympne in Kent it flew scheduled cargo trips to France and Belgium. G-AMWW Douglas DC-3 Dakota (c/n 33010) is at base in May 1970. The company ceased its operations ten years later.

Above: SEEA (South East European Airlines) flew from Athens operating local area services. SX-BSC Swearingen SA226TC Metro II (c/n TC-301) lands at base in June 1993. The following year the company ceased operations.

Below: SEA – Shannon Executive Aviation Ltd – was, as the name implies, an Irish executive/air taxi operator based in the far west at Shannon. EI-BRI Swearingen SA226TC Metro II (c/n TC-386) is at Liverpool–Speke for a horse race in April 1986. During 1990 the company suspended operations.

Above: SAC (Servicios Aereos Cochabamba) flew this single Curtiss C-46D Commando CP1655 (c/n 33294) on ad hoc cargo flights around Bolivia. It is at base in November 1992. Services were suspended in 1994.

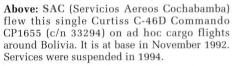

Above: Air cargo operator **Sundance Airlines** was based in San Juan, Puerto Rico. It flew an all-piston-engined fleet. N152PA Convair CV-240 (c/n 279) is at Tucson in September 1988. The following year operations were suspended.

Left: **Satena** (Servicio de Aeronavegación a Territorios Nacionales) of Colombia is not just an airline but is part of the Colombian Air Force. Its task is to fly to locations that need an air service but cannot always support a commercial one. The aircraft fly with military serial numbers. FAC 1108 Avro (HS) 748 Srs 2B-371 (c/n 1776) is at Villavicencio in November 1992.

Above: Seen at Medellin, Colombia, in November 1992, is HK1212 Douglas DC-3 Dakota (c/n 4987) of **Sadelca** (Sociedad Aerea del Caqueta). The company has a fleet of four Dakotas, two are freighters.

Below: The style of the livery of **Scanair** shows it to be part of SAS; the charter arm. SE-DHT Douglas DC-10-10 (c/n 47833) is at Miami in June 1989. At the beginning of 1994 it merged with Conair to form Premiair.

Above: **SAM Colombia** is based in the well known city of Medellin. Passenger services are flown around the country. HK3151X Boeing 727-51 (c/n 19122) departs Bogota in November 1992.

Above: **Slate Falls Airways** of Sioux Lookout, Ontario, flies on floats/wheels/skis depending on the season and location. Taking fishermen to remote lodges is one of its main activities. C-FITS de Havilland (Canada) DHC3 Otter (c/n 90) is at base, June 1990.

Below: Los Angeles-based **Spirit of America Airlines** had a fleet of freight aircraft available for ad hoc charters. N668F Lockheed L-188AF Electra (c/n 1144) is at Tucson in September 1988. The following year services were suspended.

Below: From its formation in 1947 Miami-based **Southern Air Transport** has flown cargo charters worldwide. N520SJ Lockheed L-100-30 (c/n 4299) is at base in August 1986.

Right: Southwest Airlines of Dallas, Texas, is one of the fastest-growing airlines in the world. With low fares, high frequency and no frills, but a great sense of fun, it sets standards of turn-around times that other carriers can only dream about. N103SW Boeing 737-2H4 (c/n 23109) is at Phoenix–Sky Harbor, Arizona, in September 1988. (See Special Colour Schemes, p. 143.)

Above: Caracas is the base of **Servivensa**, a subsidiary of Avensa. The airline flies scheduled services around South America and to the U.S.A. YV610C Douglas DC-3C Dakota (c/n 9894) is at Kavac in central Venezuela on a sightseeing trip to Angel Falls in November 1992.

Below: Flying with four leased TU-154s is **SAN**, an airline from the city of Karaganda in the republic of Kazakhstan. RA85824 Tupolev TU-154M (c/n 769) is at the passenger terminal at Sharjah, U.A.E., in March 1997.

Above: Travel club **Sierra Trans Air** flew this Boeing 720-022 N7225U (c/n 18078). It is seen at Boeing Field, Washington, in September 1984. By the end of the decade it had been sold to Zaire, withdrawn from use and reduced to spares.

Above: Sierra Leone Airways was based in the capital of Freetown. This small west African country has never had major air transport systems. 9L-LAD de Havilland DH114 Heron 1B (c/n 14025) is at London–Gatwick for maintenance in August 1973. Note that this mark of Heron has a fixed undercarriage. Operations were suspended in 1987. (*J.D.S.*)

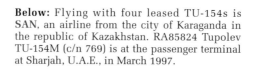

Below: Russian carrier **Special Cargo Airlines** is based at Kaluga. It flies a mixed fleet of helicopters/passenger/cargo aircraft. RA26172 Antonov AN-26B (c/n 13906) sits awaiting a load at Sharjah in March 1997.

Below: Sunaire Express flies services from its base in the Virgin Islands around the Caribbean. N929MA de Havilland (Canada) DHC6 Twin Otter 300 (c/n 500) departs San Juan in November 1992.

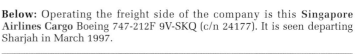

Below: Operating the freight side of the company is this **Singapore Airlines Cargo** Boeing 747-212F 9V-SKQ (c/n 24177). It is seen departing Sharjah in March 1997.

Above: Signal Hill Airlines did not exist, so what was a 707 of theirs doing on the ramp at Long Beach in October 1976? At the time this Boeing 707-331 N9230Z (c/n 17683) was registered to Aerotron Aircraft Radio which was reducing the aircraft to spares. A staff sense of humour and the fact that Signal Hill is a district of Long Beach may be the answer to the puzzle. (*S.G.W.*)

Below: British independent airline **Transglobe** first appeared in July 1965 when Air Links was renamed. The main company task was holiday charters. G-AWGS Canadair CL44D4-1 (c/n 27) is at the company base of London–Gatwick in July 1968. It is of note that the company used the CL44 in a passenger role. At the end of November that year operations were suspended. (*S.G.W.*)

Above: TAP (Transportes Aereos Portugueses), or Air Portugal, flies scheduled passenger services to all parts of Europe, Africa, North and South America. CS-TEB Lockheed L-1011 TriStar 500 (c/n 1240) arrives at London–Heathrow in October 1993.

Below: French airline **Trans Alsace** was based at Basle–Mulhouse, a truly international airport: one half is in Switzerland! F-GHOO McDonnell Douglas MD-83 (c/n 49985) lands at London–Gatwick in August 1993. The carrier suspended services in June 1994.

Below: Tolair Services flies mostly freight with a fleet of propliners. N780T Douglas DC-3 Dakota (c/n 20865) is on the move at the company base of San Juan, Puerto Rico, in November 1992.

Above: Transamerica Airlines took its title in 1979, having been TIA before that. It flew both passenger and cargo charters having an equal size split of each in the fleet. N103TV Douglas DC-10-30 (c/n 46802) is at Manchester–Ringway in October 1981. The airline suspended services in September 1986. (*P.E.P.*)

Above: Part of the KLM group, **Transavia** has for over thirty years been flying charters and leasing its fleet to other airlines. PH-TVR Boeing 737-2K2 (c/n 22025) lands at Athens in June 1993.

Right: Argentine cargo airline **TAR** – Transporte Aereo Rioplatense – started revenue services in 1971; it flew worldwide freight operations. LV-JTN Canadair CL44D4-6 (c/n 34) climbs out of London–Gatwick in August 1973. Services were suspended in 1989. (*J.D.S.*)

Above: New York-based **Tower Air** has grown since its formation in 1982 to have a fleet of twenty jumbos with one class seating to fit in 480 passengers. Both scheduled and charter flights are flown on an international basis. N603FF Boeing 747-130 (c/n 19746) arrives at Athens in June 1993.

Below: One of the many propliner operators in Villavicencio, Colombia, is **Tagua** (Taxi Aereo del Guaviare). As the name says, its main task is air taxi. Douglas DC-3 Dakota HK3349 (c/n 11825) is at base in November 1992. This particular aircraft is a freighter.

Above: Transoriente Colombia Douglas DC-3 Dakota HK2213 (c/n 11752) arrives with a passenger load at company H.Q. of Villavicencio in November 1992. The carrier, unlike a lot of airlines in this location, has furnished the exterior with a very smart livery.

Above: Seen at Opa Locka, Florida, in store without engines is Douglas DC-8-21 N821F (c/n 45433) in the livery of **Transoceanic Airways**. The operator had not started revenue services. Photographed in May 1989.

Below: Taxsur (Transportes Aereos del Sur) was a small Bogota-based Colombian freight operator. HK3740X Convair CV-580 (c/n 145), their largest aircraft, is at base in November 1992. The carrier suspended services in 1995.

Below: Taerco (Taxi Aereo Colombiano) is yet another Villavicencio-based air taxi line. This Douglas DC-3 Dakota HK1315 (c/n 4307) is the carrier's sole freighter. It is at base, November 1992.

Below: TEA U.K. (Trans European Airways) was an associate of TEA Belgium, with scheduled passenger flights being flown to Europe from U.K. bases. G-BTEB Boeing 737-2M8 (c/n 21736) is under tow at Manchester–Ringway in March 1989. The Birmingham-based company ceased services in September 1991.

Above: Austrian carrier **Tyrolean Airways** flies scheduled services around Europe from its base in Innsbruck. OE-LLS de Havilland (Canada) DHC7 Dash 7 (c/n 22) is about to touch down at Zürich in August 1987.

Below: Tatra Air is an airline from the new republic of Slovakia. This country was the result of a peaceful split with the Czechs. OM-UGU Saab SF340B (c/n 340B-163) is at Zürich in April 1996. 'OM' is the new country prefix. (*P.E.P.*)

Above: **Tala Colombia** (Transportes Aereos Latinoamericanos) flies an example each of a DC-3 and a C-46, both in the freight role. HK2581 Douglas DC-3 Dakota (c/n 27006) is at the carrier's base of Bogota in November 1992. Note the nose art on this aircraft.

Below: **Trans Ocean Airways** took that name in July 1989 when Gulf Air of New Iberia, Louisiana, changed its title. N794AL Douglas DC-8-63 (c/n 45923) departs Manchester–Ringway in July 1989. It was to be a short-lived change as early the following year services were suspended.

Above: **Transamazonica Colombia** (Transporte Aereo de la Amazonia) is yet another Villavicencio-based propliner operator. HK3359 Douglas DC-3 Dakota (c/n 34295) is one third of the company fleet, seen at base in November 1992.

Above: **Trado** – Trans Dominican Airways operates passenger and freight services from the capital, Santo Domingo. HI-594CT Convair CV-440 (c/n 118) is a passenger craft with forty-four seats. It is at base in November 1992.

Right: The proportion of civil to military aircraft that is preserved is very low. Those that are can show off colour schemes and airline names no longer to be seen. CF-THI Vickers Viscount 757 (c/n 270) is in the livery in which it served **Trans-Canada Air Lines**. It is preserved in the national collection at Rockcliffe, Ontario. The airline changed its name to Air Canada in 1964. The photograph was taken in July 1986.

Above: Transwede of Stockholm fly holiday charters. SE-DHG McDonnell Douglas MD-87 (c/n 49389) lands at Manchester–Ringway in September 1996. The following month the company changed its name to Blue Scandinavia.

Below: Trans-Air-Link is one of the last of what used to be many propliner operators at Miami. N779TA Douglas DC-6A (c/n 45529) lands at base in June 1989. Few of the smaller cargo lines tramping around the Caribbean spend a lot on corporate image.

Above: Irish charter airline **Translift Airways** is a member of the All Leisure Group. EI-TLC Douglas DC-8-71 (c/n 45995) is at Manchester–Ringway in July 1993. The '70' series DC-8s are '60' series re-engined with CFM-56s. The carrier became TransAer on 1 May 1997.

Above: Trippier Air Service is one of many small charter air taxi operators flying off Canadian lakes. C-FLUA de Havilland (Canada) DHC2 Beaver (c/n 1318) is seen on Lac Seul, Ontario, in June 1990.

Below: Tavic (Transporte Aereos Virgen de Carmen) is a Bolivian cargo line based at Cochabamba. CP1280 Curtiss C-46F Commando (c/n 22569) is at base, November 1992. This aircraft, the carrier's only one, has a very smart livery.

Below: TACA International Airlines of El Salvador is the national airline with a history dating back to 1939. Passenger services are flown to South/Central/North America. YS-08C Boeing 737-2A1 (c/n 21599) is at Miami in October 1981.

Above: Flying scheduled passenger services from its base in the city of Tunis is **Tunis air**. Established fifty years ago it flies around North Africa, Europe and the Middle East. TS-IOC Boeing 737-2H3 (c/n 21973) is at Zürich in August 1987.

Below: TAN (Transportes Aereos Nacionales) was for many a year the main airline in Honduras with passenger services around Central America and to Miami. N88705 Boeing 727-224 (c/n 19514) is at the latter in June 1989. Two years later they merged with, and took the identity of, Sahsa, another carrier based with them at Tegucigalpa.

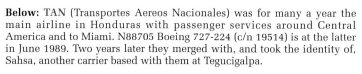

Below: For many years **Trans Continental Airlines** has been flying cargo services for the motor industry out of Detroit–Willow Run. N8052U Douglas DC-8F-54 (c/n 46009) is at base, in its very smart livery, in June 1990.

Above: Looking after the freight side of the operation was **TAN – Carga**. HR-TNT Lockheed L-188AF Electra (c/n 1060) lands at Miami in June 1989. It also merged with Sahsa.

Below: Thai Airways International is one of the fast-growing Asian airlines. With a fleet of very new aircraft and perhaps the world's best cabin service, it flies worldwide from the capital Bangkok. HS-TIC Airbus A310-204 (c/n 424) is at Phuket in November 1989 on an internal service.

Above: Colombian cargo carrier **Tampa** (Transportes Aereos Mercantiles Panamericanos) flies an all-jet fleet of 707/DC-8s from its Medellin base. HK3333X Boeing 707-321C (c/n 18714) lands on a regular flight at Miami in June 1989.

Above: Tarom (Transporturile Aeriene Romane) has been since its foundation in 1954 the national airline of Romania. Scheduled passenger and freight services cover much of the world. YR-TPJ Tupolev TU-154B-2 (c/n 408) is at London–Heathrow in May 1988. As with most eastern European airlines the old Russian aircraft types will be replaced by western designs.

Right: French scheduled carrier **TAT** got its initials by being Touraine Air Transport. In 1984 it was renamed Transport Aérien Transregional. Services are flown around Europe. F-GDUS Fokker F28 Fellowship 2000 (c/n 11053) shows its striking livery at Zürich in August 1987. Now part-owned by BA a number of aircraft fly in that carrier's colours.

Above: Still flying a fleet of six cargo 707s, **TMA of Lebanon** (Trans Mediterranean Airways) plies the skies on a worldwide basis. N7095 (now OD-AGX) Boeing 707-327C (c/n 19104) is at London–Heathrow in June 1978.

Below: Transasian Airlines was a British charter company based at Luton. N762TB Boeing 707-321B (c/n 18337) is at base in May 1979. Later that year the carrier was renamed Air Intercontinental Airlines.

Above: Houston-based **Texas International** was a major U.S. domestic carrier. N94258 Convair CV-600 (c/n 119) is in store at Ryan Field, Arizona, October 1979. The airline merged into Continental in 1982.

Above: British independent **TMAC – Trans Meridian Air Cargo** – was formed in 1962 to fly freight charters. G-AXAA Canadair CL44D4-2 (c/n 18) is in the static park of an air show at North Weald in May 1972. The company was renamed British Cargo Airlines in 1979.

Below: U.S. Passenger and cargo charter operator **Trans International Airlines** flew services, with a large fleet, worldwide. N797FT Douglas DC-8-63 (c/n 46140) is at Paris–Le Bourget in May 1973. The airline was renamed Transamerica in 1979 and kept the same basic colours.

Below: Tyumenaviatrans is yet another ex-Aeroflot region forming its own airline. RA85808 Tupolev TU-154M (c/n 989) is at Moscow–Domodedovo in August 1995. As can be seen little has changed in the basic livery.

Above: A sight unthinkable only a few years ago, a **Turkmenistan Airlines** aircraft and a western design as well. EZ-A002 Boeing 737-332 (c/n 25994) lands at London–Heathrow in June 1996. Turkmenistan is one of the 'new' ex-U.S.S.R. republics.

Above: Based in Marseille, **Trans-union** was a French charter operator. F-BNUZ Douglas DC-6B (c/n 45173) is at Paris–Le Bourget in July 1970. This aircraft was used to fly the Air France night newspaper delivery contract. In September 1971 operations were transferred to Europe Aero Services.

Below: **TranStar** was the name given to Muse Air after it was taken over by Southwest. The airline flew high-frequency services in the south-west of America. N930MC McDonnell Douglas MD-82 (c/n 48056) is at Los Angeles–LAX in August 1986. The Houston-based carrier suspended services in August 1989.

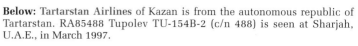

Below: **Tartarstan Airlines** of Kazan is from the autonomous republic of Tartarstan. RA85488 Tupolev TU-154B-2 (c/n 488) is seen at Sharjah, U.A.E., in March 1997.

Below: French charter line **Transvalair/Ace** flew passenger/freight/executive charters from its Paris and Caen base. F-GDPP Douglas DC-3 Dakota (c/n 9172) is at an air show at Fairford, U.K., in July 1985 to celebrate fifty years of the Dakota.

Above: **Trinity Air Bahamas** was based in the capital, Nassau. The fleet consisted of two aircraft. N1288L Douglas DC-9-32 (c/n 47443) is at Miami in April 1994. The following month the carrier ceased operations.

Above: U.K. independent carrier **Titan Airways** is a commuter line based at Stansted. G-ZAPD Short SD360-300 (c/n SH3741) is at base in May 1995.

Right: Based at Palma, Majorca, was Spanish charter airline **Transeuropa**. EC-BRX Sud Aviation SE210 Caravelle 11R (c/n 261) is at base in November 1973. The carrier was integrated into Aviaco in 1982.

Above: **Turkish Airlines** – THY (Turk Hava Yollari) is that nation's flag carrier. From Istanbul it flies services worldwide. TC-JDL Airbus A340-311 (c/n 057) lands at London–Heathrow in July 1995.

Below: Russian start-up airline **Transaero Airlines** is one of the first to have a largely western-built fleet. EI-CLM Boeing 757-28A (c/n 24367) is at the company base of Moscow–Sheremetyevo in September 1995.

Above: British air taxi operator **Telair Manchester Ltd** was in fact based at Liverpool–Speke. G-AXXH Britten-Norman BN2A Islander (c/n 144) is at base in July 1983. Services were suspended in 1985.

Above: **TAA** – Trans-Australian Airlines – was a Melbourne-based domestic scheduled carrier. PH-EXB (re-registered VH-TQR) Fokker F27 Friendship 600 (c/n 10441) is on the manufacturer's ramp at Schiphol in July 1970. The company was renamed Australian Airlines in 1996.

Below: **Transmeridian Hong Kong** was set up in 1975 to operate a single CL44 taken from the U.K.-based Transmeridian fleet. The airline flew cargo flights all over the Far East from Hong Kong. VR-HCC Canadair CL44D4-2 (c/n 17) is at Stansted, U.K., in May 1978. (*J.D.S.*)

Below: Palma, Majorca, was the base of Spanish holiday charter airline **TAE** (Trabajos Aeroeos y Enlaces). EC-CDC Douglas DC-8-32 (c/n 45567) is at base, November 1974. The carrier ceased operations during 1981.

Above: Turkish holiday charter airline **Torosair** flew a fleet of six 727s from its base at Istanbul. TC-AJV Boeing 727-247 (c/n 20265) is at Manchester–Ringway in July 1989. Later that year operations were suspended. (*J.D.S.*)

Below: TNT is a worldwide parcel delivery company. The aviation service of the operation flies a fleet of BAe 146QT freighters; the QT stands for 'Quiet Trader', a reference to the low-noise signature of the aeroplane enabling it to fly night services without breaking noise regulations. G-TNTG BAe 146-300QT (c/n E3182) is at Liverpool–Speke in June 1993.

Below: Formed in 1968, **TAC Colombia** (Transportes Aereas de Cesar) flew scheduled domestic passenger services. HK1137 Fairchild F27 Friendship (c/n 40) is in store at Marana, Arizona, in October 1979. The following year the carrier's name was changed to Aerocesar.

Above: American all-cargo carrier **Tradewinds International Airlines** was the last major user of the CL44, with a fleet of five. N106BB Canadair CL44D4-2 (c/n 37) has its swing tail open on the ramp at Santo Domingo, Dominican Republic in November 1992. With the advent of the carrier operating L-1011 TriStar freight aircraft most of the CL44s are in store.

Below: Istanbul-based **Top Air** flies a mixed fleet of passenger craft from small eight-seaters to 170-place 727s. TC-IYC Boeing 727-2F2 (c/n 21260) is at Düsseldorf, July 1996. (*J.D.S.*)

Above: **Transair Sweden** was a Malmo-based charter airline owned by SAS. SE-ERL Douglas DC-7B (c/n 45346) is at London–Gatwick in August 1968. The carrier ceased operations in 1981.

Above: **Travair** was a one-aeroplane airline based in Perth, Western Australia. It flew VH-SBL Douglas DC-3 Dakota (c/n 12056). It is seen at Melbourne–Essendon in November 1986. The aircraft was sold at the end of the following year. (*R.O'B.*)

131

Right: Seen at Opa Locka, Florida, in July 1974 was this Grumman G21A Goose N2721A (c/n B-54) in the markings of **Tasman Airlines** of Australia. The following month the aircraft flew on delivery to Melbourne, by way of the U.K. In 1975 it took up the Australian registration of VH-CRL. (*S.G.W.*)

Above: In November 1970 Norwegian airline **Trans Polar** bought two Boeings from Aer Lingus. In May of the following year they were repossessed. LN-TUV Boeing 720-048 (c/n 18043) is in store on the ramp at Dublin in July 1971. (*S.G.W.*)

Above: Tour company **TBG** (Thorne Browne Group) has got this Lockheed L-1011 TriStar 1 EI-TBG (c/n 1030) in its livery. The aircraft is owned by Translift. It is seen landing at London–Gatwick in September 1996. (*S.G.W.*)

Below: **Taino Airlines** of the Dominican Republic has sub-leased for a short term this Douglas DC-10-30 F-GHOI (c/n 46870) from its owners Scribe-Airlift of Zaire. That company, too, had leased it, hence the French registration. It is seen at Frankfurt in September 1993. (*S.G.W.*)

Above: **Taesa** (Transportes Aereos Ejecutivos) of Mexico City has large fleets of both airliners and executive jets. XA-SYE Douglas DC-10-30 (c/n 46990) is on a short lease to a British holiday operator and is seen at London–Gatwick in August 1996. (*S.G.W.*)

Above: **Tulip Air** is a Dutch independent airline based at Rotterdam. PH-ATM Beechcraft Catpass 200 (King Air) (c/n BB-123) is at base in August 1995 showing off a very distinctive livery. (*P.E.P.*)

Below: **Trans Caribbean** was a U.S. scheduled carrier serving such places as Puerto Rico and the U.S. Virgin Islands from its New York base. N8783R Douglas DC-8-54 (c/n 45684) is at New York–J.F.K. in August 1970. The airline was taken over by American Airlines in May 1971. (*S.G.W.*)

Below: Brazilian airline **TABA** (Transportes Aereos de Bacia Amazonica) of Belem is a regional commuter line. G-SSHH BAe 146-100 (c/n E1002) is seen at the Paris Air Show, Le Bourget, in May 1983. The company had its own two 146s delivered later that year.

Above: Turku Air is from Turku in Finland and flies commuter services with a small fleet. OH-PNU Piper PA31 Navajo Chieftain (c/n 31-7752027) is on the ramp at Tallinn, Estonia, for an international service in May 1995. (*J.D.S.*)

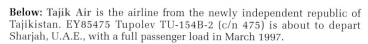

Below: Tajik Air is the airline from the newly independent republic of Tajikistan. EY85475 Tupolev TU-154B-2 (c/n 475) is about to depart Sharjah, U.A.E., with a full passenger load in March 1997.

Above: Trans World Express is the commuter feeder for TWA. N3107P Swearingen SA227AC Metro III (c/n AC-496) is at Washington National in May 1989. The airline owning this aeroplane was Pocono Airlines with all its fleet in T.W. Express service and colours. Pocono suspended services in January 1990.

Below: The **Tashkent Aircraft Production Corporation** is the flying division of the factory that manufactured many Russian aircraft. It flies cargo charters as well as corporate work. UK76427 Ilyushin IL-76TD (c/n 1013406207) is at Sharjah in March 1997 operating a freight flight.

Below: TWA – Trans World Airlines – has a history going back to 1930. It, with Pan Am, was the American flag carrier operating a worldwide service. N795TW Boeing 707-131B (c/n 18758) is seen landing at Miami in October 1981.

Above: TAM (Transportes Aereos Regionais) is a Brazilian scheduled passenger airline based in São Paulo. PT-MRO Fokker 100 (c/n 11470) is at Rio–Santo Dumont airport in April 1995. (*R.O'B.*)

Above: TEA Switzerland is an all-737 passenger airline based at Basle. HB-IID Boeing 737-3Y0 (c/n 24255) is at Zürich in April 1996. (*J.D.S.*)

133

Right: UPS – United Parcel Service – is one of America's and the world's prime movers of small packages. With a large fleet of 200-plus jets it was the launch customer for both 757/767 freight variants. N936UP Boeing 727-108C (c/n 19503) is at Miami in April 1994.

Above: Universal (Transportes Aereos Universal) is a La Paz-based Bolivian meat freight carrier. It flies freshly killed cattle carcasses from the lowland farms to the city of La Paz at 12,000 feet above sea level. CP746 Curtiss C-46A Commando (c/n 26417) starts its engines at base in November 1992. The company was renamed SAO during 1994.

Below: The **United States Postal Service** needs to fly the mail around that vast country. N435EX Boeing 727-51C (c/n 19288) is at San Juan, Puerto Rico, in November 1992. It awaits the night run to the hub at Indianapolis via Miami. The aeroplane is owned by Emery Worldwide but is operated by Ryan International.

Above: Based in the California state capital of Sacramento, **Union Flights** flies freight to feed the big carrier hubs. N544Y de Havilland (Canada) DHC4A Caribou (c/n 241) is at base in September 1988. Very few commercial operators fly the Caribou; this S.T.O.L. (short take-off and landing) workhorse prop was sold mainly to the military.

Above: UTA – Union de Transports Aériens – was France's largest independent airline flying scheduled services to many points on a worldwide basis. F-BLNE Douglas DC-8-62 (c/n 45917) is at Paris–Le Bourget in July 1970. The carrier was taken over by Air France during 1992.

Below: Unifly Express was an Italian charter company based in Rome. EI-BTX McDonnell Douglas MD-83 (c/n 49660) is at Luton, U.K., in July 1988. The carrier suspended operations during 1990.

Below: To this first aircraft **Universal Airlines** added four more of the same type. N861TA Douglas DC-6A/B (c/n 43522) is at the company base of Detroit–Willow Run in June 1990. The all-freight operator only flew for two years, services being suspended in 1992.

Above: Spanish holiday charter company **Universair** had a fleet of three 737s. From its Palma, Majorca, base it flew to the Spanish sunspots. EC-EGQ Boeing 737-3Q8 (c/n 23506) is on the move on a wet August day at Manchester–Ringway in 1989. The airline merged into Meridiana during May 1991. (*J.D.S.*)

Above: **United Airlines** is one of the world's largest carriers with both U.S. domestic and international worldwide passenger services. N768UA Boeing 777-222 (c/n 26919) lands at London–Heathrow in July 1995 in the company's current livery.

Above: Showing that Russia knows how to paint airliners is **Ural Airlines** of Ekaterinburg. RA85814 Tupolev TU-154M (c/n 994) is in the static at the Moscow Trade Air Show at Zhukovsky, August 1995.

Below: **Uzbekistan Airways** flies from the capital, Tashkent, of this ex-U.S.S.R. country with a stunning livery. F-OGQZ Airbus A310-324 (c/n 576) arrives at London–Heathrow in June 1996. Most of the airline's fleet are Russian aircraft but western airliners are to be found on the prestige routes.

Below: **USAir Express** is the commuter feeder for USAir. N3049D Swearingen SA227AC Metro III (c/n AC-485) is on an international service to Hamilton, Ontario, in June 1990.

Below: **USAir** used to be known as Allegheny until 1979. The company flies to destinations all over America with a fleet of several hundred aircraft. N177US BAe 146-200A (c/n E2039) is at Orange County, California, in September 1988. During 1997 the name will change to U.S. Airways and a new livery will appear.

Above: **United Express** feeds the commuters to the main United hubs. N270UE Embraer E120 Brasilia (c/n 120026) lands at Santa Barbara, California, in September 1988 in the carrier's previous colours.

Above: Based in the capital, Kampala, **Uganda Airlines** no longer operates long-range aircraft. The current fleet is just three aircraft, two of which are 737s. Dating back to long-range days is 5X-UAC Boeing 707-351C (c/n 18747). It is seen at Stansted, U.K., in May 1986.

Right: Brazil's main airline **Varig** (Viacão Aerea Rio – Grandense), like a number on that continent, has a long history, in this case back to 1927. It flies services to worldwide destinations from its base at Rio de Janeiro. PP-VOP McDonnell Douglas MD-11 (c/n 48434) arrives at London–Heathrow in July 1995.

Above: Atlanta, Georgia-based **Valujet** grew at such a rapid pace it could hardly keep up with itself. The carrier offered low fares with no frills. N1273L Douglas DC-9-32 (c/n 47321) shows off its livery at Tampa, Florida, in April 1994. The airline was shut down by the F.A.A. following a fatal crash but has been allowed to restart.

Below: **Viscount Air Service** is a Tucson, Arizona-based charter company with a fleet of thirteen 737s. Five of these are fitted with executive interiors. N221AW Boeing 737-247 (c/n 20125) is at Orlando, Florida, in April 1994. In January 1996 the company filed for protection from creditors under Chapter 11. It is continuing operations.

Above: **Viasa** (Venezolana Internacional de Aviación) was the government-owned flag carrier of Venezuela. It was formed as late as 1961 and flew international services from Caracas. YV-138C Douglas DC-10-30 (c/n 46557) is at base in November 1992. With losses of over $100 million the carrier was shut down in January 1997.

Above: **Viva Air** (Vuelos Internacionales de Vacaciones) is a charter line owned by the Spanish carrier Iberia. EC-EHX Boeing 737-3A4 (c/n 23752) lands at Manchester–Ringway in August 1990.

Below: **Vintage Airways** was a trip into the past. It flew two Dakotas from Kissimmee, Florida, on services to Key West in the style and comfort of 1945; other charters were flown as required. N22RB Douglas DC-3 Dakota (c/n 4926) is at base in April 1994. The style of livery gives away the fact it was part of the Virgin Group. Regrettably the demand was not high enough and in October 1994 the operation was suspended.

Below: **Volga-Dnepr Airlines** is the leader in the carriage of oversize items with a fleet of IL-76/AN-124s based at Ulyanovsk. There is a tie-up with U.K. airline Heavylift. RA82078 Antonov AN-124-100 Ruslan (c/n 9773054559153) is on the cargo ramp at Sharjah, U.A.E., in March 1997.

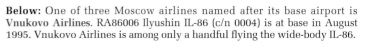

Below: One of three Moscow airlines named after its base airport is **Vnukovo Airlines**. RA86006 Ilyushin IL-86 (c/n 0004) is at base in August 1995. Vnukovo Airlines is among only a handful flying the wide-body IL-86.

Above: Veteran Airlines of Simferopol, Ukraine, has an associate company with the same name based in Moscow, Russia. The fleet of both companies is made up of the IL-76 freight aircraft. UR-76684 Ilyushin IL-76MD of the Ukraine company is at Moscow–Zhukovsky in August 1995.

Below: With the Virgin name being so high profile the company is able to franchise it to other airlines. Such a partnership was **Virgin/SEEA** (South East European Airlines). It operated this Boeing 737-4Y0 G-UKLB (c/n 24344). It is seen at the SEEA base, Athens, in June 1993.

Above: Virgin Atlantic is still a relatively small airline in world terms but has a very high public awareness factor due to the company founder and head Richard Branson's love of publicity. The airline flies to the U.S.A. and the Far East with more routes due. Scheduled passenger flights together with holiday charters from Virgin's own travel company occupy the fleet of 747/A340s. G-VFLY Airbus A340-311 (c/n 058) lands at London–Heathrow in July 1995.

Below: VI (Virgin Island) Seaplane Shuttle offered the best way to travel around the U.S. Virgin Islands. N653SS Grumman G73 Mallard (c/n J-53) powers its way ashore at St Thomas in April 1989. Operations were suspended in June 1992. (*S.G.W.*)

Above: VASP (Viacão Aerea São Paulo) is based in Brazil's second city flying scheduled passenger services around the country and to North and South America. PP-SOC Boeing 737-33A (c/n 24790) is at the company base, São Paulo, in January 1992. (*R.O'B.*)

Above: Venus Airlines is a Greek holiday charter carrier. EI-CLP Boeing 757-2Y0 (c/n 25268) is at Zürich in April 1996. (*P.E.P.*)

Far Right: Volare Air Transport Company of Moscow has a fleet of six aircraft of five different types, a mixture of passenger and cargo aircraft. RA65926 Tupolev TU-134A (c/n 66101) is at Moscow–Sheremetyevo in August 1995. This aircraft is on lease to Transaero Express, hence the extra markings. (*J.D.S.*)

Right: Virgin Express is the new name of Brussels-based EBA – Euro Belgian Airlines. It was taken over by the Virgin Group in 1996 and is resplendent in the new smart livery. OO-LTP Boeing 737-33A (c/n 25032) lands at Manchester–Ringway in March 1997. (*J.D.S.*)

Above: Bulgarian charter airline **VIA** flies a fleet of six TU-154s from its base in the capital, Sofia. LZ-MIG Tupolev TU-154M (c/n 840) arrives at Manchester–Ringway in March 1997.

Below: World Airways was founded in 1948 as a charter company. It flies a fleet of DC-10/MD-11s with all-one class seating. The carrier is based at Charleston, South Carolina. N107WA Douglas DC-10-30F (c/n 46836) is at Manchester–Ringway in July 1993.

Above: VLM (Vlaame Luchttransport Maatschappij) is an Antwerp, Belgium scheduled passenger airline with flights around Europe. OO-VLM Fokker 50 (c/n 20135) lands at London–City in June 1996. (*P.E.P.*)

Above: Western Express was the feeder to the main services of Western. N2685L Swearingen SA227 Metro III (c/n AC-648) is at Los Angeles–LAX in August 1986. It later became Skywest (Delta).

Below: Based at London–City, **World Airlines** operated a service to Amsterdam several times a day. Operations commenced in 1996. G-WLCY BAe 146-200A (c/n E2030) is at base in June 1996. Within one year services had been suspended. (*J.D.S.*)

Below: Worldways Canada flew charter services on a worldwide basis from its Toronto base. C-GFLG Boeing 707-365C (c/n 19416) is at Manchester–Ringway in September 1984. The airline suspended services in October 1990. (*J.D.S.*)

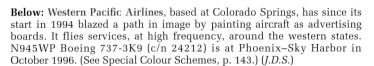

Below: Western Pacific Airlines, based at Colorado Springs, has since its start in 1994 blazed a path in image by painting aircraft as advertising boards. It flies services, at high frequency, around the western states. N945WP Boeing 737-3K9 (c/n 24212) is at Phoenix–Sky Harbor in October 1996. (See Special Colour Schemes, p. 143.) (*J.D.S.*)

Above: Wings Airways flew commuters around Pennsylvania. N414WA Britten-Norman BN2A Mk111.2 Trislander (c/n 1034) waits for its next passenger load at a night-time Philadelphia in March 1989. (*S.G.W.*)

Below: WestAir Commuter Airlines acted as a feeder for United. N634KC Short SD360 (c/n SH3646) lands at Los Angeles–LAX in September 1988. The Fresno, California-based carrier now operates Cessna Caravans for Fed-Ex.

Above: Wardair Canada grew from one D.H. Fox Moth in 1946 to twelve A310s when in January 1990 it was taken over by Canadian. The airline had flown charters on a worldwide basis. C-GXRB Douglas DC-10-30 (c/n 46976) is at London–Gatwick in July 1988.

Above: Winkies Fish/Northern Peninsula Fisheries used this Douglas DC-8F-55 N804SW (c/n 45816) for the Alaska salmon flights. It is seen at Boeing Field, Washington, in September 1984.

Below: Walsten Air Service flies from Kenora, Ontario, both from the airport and the sea plane base. It undertakes ad hoc charter work around the province. C-FOCU de Havilland (Canada) DHC2 Beaver (c/n 73) is at the S.P.B. in June 1990.

Above: Western Airlines claimed to be the oldest airline in America, going back to 1925. It flew scheduled passenger services across America. N3301 Boeing 737-347 (c/n 23181) is at Billings, Montana, in August 1986. Delta Airlines took over the company in April 1987.

Above: Wien Air Alaska flew scheduled passenger services around the state and to the 'lower 48'. N275WC Boeing 727-277 (c/n 20549) is at Seattle–Tacoma in September 1984. Later that year flying operations were suspended.

Right: Xiamen Airlines is a Chinese mainland operator with a fleet of seventeen 737/757s. B2819 Boeing 757-25C (c/n 25898) lands at Hong Kong in February 1996. (*J.D.S.*)

Above: Young Air Cargo was a Belgian company based at Gosselies. It was set up in 1975 by the ex-chief pilot of TEA. XM497/OO-YCF Bristol Britannia 253 (c/n 13509) is at Stansted, U.K., in August 1976, still in the basic R.A.F. colours. This airframe was purchased to act as a spares supply to the operational fleet of four. The company moved to jets in 1977 and ceased flying in 1979.

Above: ZAS (Zarkani Aviation Services) Airline of Egypt was set up in Cairo in 1982 to fly cargo services on a scheduled basis to Europe; passenger flights followed. SU-DAB Boeing 707-328C (c/n 19521) departs London–Gatwick in July 1988. The company suspended services in 1995.

Above: Yemenia – Yemen Airways flies from the capital, Sana'a, on scheduled services around the Middle East and to Europe, as well as domestic operations. F-0HPS Airbus A310-325 (c/n 704) arrives at Sharjah, U.A.E., on a passenger flight in March 1997. This carrier was the airline from North Yemen; following the civil war and unification of the North and South this is the carrier for the whole nation.

Below: Zambian Airways was the sole airline flying scheduled long-haul services in that country. N3016Z Douglas DC-10-30 (c/n 48266) lands at London–Heathrow on a flight from Lusaka in September 1993. The carrier suspended operations in December 1994.

Above: Zantop International Airlines was set up in 1972 to fly automobile industry cargo on a contract basis. N7529U Convair CV-640 (c/n 58) is at the company base of Detroit–Willow Run in June 1990. Flying operations were closed down in May 1997.

Above: Zuliana de Aviación is a Venezuelan passenger airline based at Maracaibo. Services are flown, both domestic and international. YV-462C Boeing 727-2B7 (c/n 20303) is at Caracas in November 1992.

Below: Zimex Aviation of Zürich flies a mix of aircraft in a variety of tasks. They include passengers/parcels/executives. These operations take place in many locations, especially Africa. HB-ILG Lockheed L-100-30 Hercules (c/n 35C-4698) is at East Midlands–Castle Donington in June 1988.

Below: 4 Island Air Services flew scheduled flights around the Caribbean from the company base in Antigua. V2-LAG Britten-Norman BN2A Islander (c/n 163) is at base in June 1983. The company was a subsidiary of LIAT and was absorbed into it in 1986. (*R.O'B.*)

Special Colour Schemes

It has long been the practice of airlines to present to its passengers an aeroplane in special markings to commemorate a unique event. These have ranged from an anniversary to a sporting event at the carrier's home base. In years past these have generally been low key markings taking the form of an extra logo on top of the carrier's regular colour scheme. However, the most recent trend has been for full blown paintings that have little or nothing to do with the aircraft's normal livery. The schemes have celebrated such things as a new route that the carrier's flies or quite simply to advertise a product. This tailpiece gives a small snapshot of some of the colour schemes that can be or have been seen at airports worldwide. Compare and contrast them with the 'normal' colours in the main section.

Left: America West Airlines of Phoenix, Arizona, has produced some spectacular colour schemes to commemorate various places, events and sports teams. N902AW Boeing 757-257 (c/n 23322) is *Teamwork for the company staff*; Phoenix–Sky Harbor, October 1996. (*J.D.S.*)

Above: N916AW Boeing 757-23A (c/n 24291) is *Arizona*. This is based on the state flag and is the airline's home state; Phoenix–Sky Harbor, October 1996. (*J.D.S.*)

Above: N915AW Boeing 757-225 (c/n 22209) is *Nevada*. Again based on the state flag it carries the state motto 'Battle Born'; Phoenix–Sky Harbor, October 1996. (*J.D.S.*)

Above: N905AW Boeing 757-257 (c/n 23567) is *Ohio*. Named *City of Columbus* after the state capital, it features the stars and bars of the U.S. flag; Phoenix–Sky Harbor, October 1996. (*J.D.S.*)

Left: N904AW Boeing 757-257 (c/n 23566) is *Diamond Backs*. This is to commemorate the fact the airline is the official carrier for the baseball team from Phoenix of that name; Phoenix–Sky Harbor, October 1996. (*J.D.S.*)

Above: America West N907AW Boeing 757-225 (c/n 22691) is *Phoenix Suns*. This is another sports team, in this case a basketball one; Phoenix–Sky Harbor, October 1996. (*J.D.S.*)

Above: Crossair again in special colours. These were to commemorate the 700th anniversary of the Swiss Federation. The aircraft HB-AHD Saab SF340A (c/n 018) is painted in markings designed by a ten-year-old Swiss schoolboy. It is landing at Manchester–Ringway in June 1995 on a normal scheduled flight. (*J.D.S.*)

Below: Ryanair with Christmas cheer. The nose of this Boeing 737-204 EI-CJF (c/n 22967) has had a white beard and red hat added for the festive season. It is seen landing at Manchester–Ringway in December 1994. Note this is Ryanair's old-style livery; see main section for the current.

Above: One of the cargo tasks Manx Airways has is the carriage of Royal Mail overnight to the sorting hubs. To advertise the Royal Mail Special Service and its Datapost this Shorts SD360-100 G-RMSS (special registration for the job) (c/n SH3604) is at Liverpool–Speke in April 1986.

Above: Major events at an airline's home base can trigger a special marking. In 1986 Expo '86, a world fair, was held in Vancouver. Canadian Pacific Douglas DC-10-10 N1836U (c/n 47968) was a flying advertisement for it as it flew the world. Seen at Toronto, July 1986.

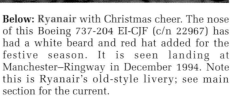

Below: SAS McDonnell Douglas MD-87 SE-DIP (c/n 53010) arrives at London–Heathrow in July 1996. It advertised 'Copenhagen '96', a city festival. Note the colours normal to the nose on SAS have been removed.

Below: Irish independent Ryanair has painted this Boeing 737-204 EI-CJE (c/n 22639) in the colours of British car maker Jaguar. The rear fuselage is British racing green. The aircraft is seen at Birmingham–Elmdon (home city of the British motor industry) in November 1996. The carrier has promised more flying adverts.

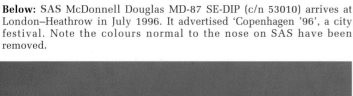

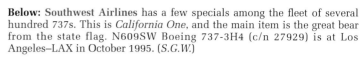

Below: **Southwest Airlines** has a few specials among the fleet of several hundred 737s. This is *California One*, and the main item is the great bear from the state flag. N609SW Boeing 737-3H4 (c/n 27929) is at Los Angeles–LAX in October 1995. (*S.G.W.*)

Above: Canadian Pacific became **Canadian**, and this Douglas DC-10-30 C-FCRE (c/n 47868) is called *Spirit of Canada* and is covered in signatures of the airline's employees. It is seen landing at London–Heathrow in June 1996.

Below: Each year Norwegian airline **Braathens** selects a 'Sommerflyet' or summer plane; it is then painted with characters from children's story books. LN-BRX Boeing 737-505 (c/n 25797) arrives at London–Gatwick in August 1993.

Above: **Western Pacific** seems to have every aeroplane in a different livery. The company's idea is for flying billboards to advertise things. Fox TV is using Boeing 737-301 N949WP (c/n 23230) to promote the animated TV show *The Simpsons*. It is at Phoenix–Sky Harbor in October 1996. (*J.D.S.*)

Below: Owned by **Sinclair Air Services** this Boeing 720-022 N7224U (c/n 18077) is in the colours of the Bee Gees, a popular 1960s/1970s rock music combo. It has on the tail *The Tour 79* and drawings of the group members. On the cabin roof is the phrase *Spirits having flown*, the latest disc being promoted by the group on the tour. The interior was an executive fit and had been used by other beat groups for touring, such as Led Zeppelin. It is seen after the tour at Marana, Arizona, in October 1979.

Above: **Western Pacific** is here advertising its own low 'Super Summer Saver' fares. N962WP Boeing 737-3Y0 (c/n 23748) is at Phoenix–Sky Harbor, October 1996. (*J.D.S.*)

Above: 1976 saw America celebrate its 200th birthday. This event was marked with special colour schemes on many U.S.A.F. aircraft. The airlines were not to be left out as this **Eastern Airlines** Lockheed L-188A Electra N5517 (c/n 1023) shows with its nose art work. It is seen at New York–La Guardia in June 1976. (*R.O'B.*)

Above: Mexican airline **Allegro Air** of Monterrey has included in their fleet mix three baby DC-9s. XA-SPA Douglas DC-9-14 (c/n 45698) is in the standard dark green and has *Abaco*, a finance company, along the cabin roof. It is seen at Orlando, Florida, in October 1995. (*J.D.S.*)

Above: A Swiss travel company had this **Crossair** McDonnell Douglas MD-82 HB-IUH (c/n 53150) painted in the colours of McDonald's, the fast-food chain. It was for charters to the Mediterranean from Zürich and Geneva; some flights even served hamburgers! It is seen landing at Manchester–Ringway in June 1996 on a football charter. (*J.D.S.*)

Bibliography

Chillon, J., Dubois, J.P. & Wegg J., *French Postwar Transport Aircraft*, Air Britain, 1980.

Eastwood, Tony & Roach, John, *Piston Engine Airliner Production List* (1991); *Jet Airliner Production List* (1992); *Turbo Prop Airliner Production List* (1994), The Aviation Hobby Shop, London

Gradidge, J.M.G., *The Douglas DC-3 and its Predecessors*, Air Britain, 1984

Klee, Ulrich, *J.P. Airline Fleets*, Bucher & Co., Zürich

Proctor, John, *Convair 880 & 990*, World Transport Press, Miami, 1996

Magazines: *Airliners, Aviation Letter, Propliner, & World Airline Fleets News*